CLARK E. MOUSTAKAS

is a faculty member at the merrill-palmer institute in detroit, and is involved in several community projects.

he is the author of numerous books, including Personal Growth, Individuality and Encounter, Creativity and Conformity, Psychotherapy with Children, *and* Loneliness.

loneliness
and love

clark e. moustakas

PRENTICE-HALL, INC. Englewood Cliffs, New Jersey

A SPECTRUM BOOK

Library of Congress Cataloging in Publication Data

Moustakas, Clark E
   Loneliness and love.

   (A Spectrum book)
   Includes bibliographies.
   1. Loneliness. I. Title.
BF575.L7M64   128   72–161
ISBN 0–13–540252–2
ISBN 0–13–540245–X (pbk.)

Grateful acknowledgment is made to the following for permission to use quotations appearing in this book: Grosset & Dunlap, Inc., and Peter Owen, Ltd., for *A Death in the Family* by James Agee, copyright © 1957 by The James Agee Trust; Grove Press, Inc., and Souvenir Press Ltd., London, for *Joy: Expanding Human Awareness* by William C. Schutz, copyright © 1967 by William C. Schutz; McGraw-Hill Book Company for *Soul on Ice* by Eldridge Cleaver, copyright © 1968 by Eldridge Cleaver; Pflaum/Standard Publishing Company for *What Counts Is Life* by Thiago de Mello, translated by Gertrude Pax; Random House, Inc., for *The Grass Harp* by Truman Capote, *The Method of Zen* by Eugen Herrigel, and *Knots* by R. D. Laing; and the Unitarian Universalist Association for *The Sound of Silence* by Raymond John Baughan.

"Loneliness and Solitude" and "Loneliness and Encounter" originally appeared in *Individuality and Encounter* by Clark E. Moustakas and have been revised with the permission of the publisher, Howard A. Doyle, for use in this volume. An earlier version of the chapter "Loneliness and Love" appeared in *Experiences in Being*, edited by Bernice Marshall, and has been revised with the permission of Brooks/Cole Publishing Co. for use in this volume.

---

10 9 8 7 6 5 4 3 2 1

Prentice-Hall International, Inc. (*London*)
Prentice-Hall of Australia, Pty. Ltd. (*Sydney*)
Prentice-Hall of Canada, Ltd. (*Toronto*)
Prentice-Hall of India Private Limited (*New Delhi*)
Prentice-Hall of Japan, Inc. (*Tokyo*)

FOR WENDY

flower of life
radiating love
through loneliness and joy
through laughter and tears

contents

preface

Loneliness and Love was not written as a book. It grew out of journeys into myself, searches that were touched off by moments of joy and beauty and wonder, by the sudden awareness of a poignant or crucial meaning in my communications and relationships with others, and by crises in which I witnessed and experienced sickness and death, deceit and betrayal, the shattering of trust, and the diminishing of the human spirit. I found that through solitude and meditation, through silence and dialogue with my self and with nature I could savor the aesthetic meaning of life in art, in music, in literature, in human encounter. I could regain a true sense of myself and return with strength and determination to continue to live in accordance with human values. Thus I give thanks to myself for having the guts to trust my own senses to choose, to decide, to act and for having the courage to keep alive my faith in human potentiality and my belief in and love for mankind.

Of course, a number of persons have supported and affirmed me and in other ways contributed to the creation of *Loneliness and Love*, especially my family, friends, students, and individuals I have come to know through intensive group experiences. I wish to express my appreciation of Mavis Wolfe both in her typing of the original manuscripts and in her presence throughout.

We are speaking of love. A leaf, a handful of seed—
    begin with these, learn a little what it is to love.
First, a leaf, a fall of rain, then someone to receive
    what a leaf has taught you, what a fall of
    rain has ripened.
No easy process, understand; it could take a
    lifetime, it has mine, and still I've never mastered it—
I only know how true it is:
    that love is a chain of love,
    as nature is a chain of life.
                    —Truman Capote, *The Grass Harp*

1 | *one to self:*
the battle to be

Every once in a while I awaken to the reality that I'm all I've got. This awareness is usually thrust upon me when the spirit of my life is broken, when the person who I am is clearly not being received, when I am being judged, examined, questioned. There is a force, a vitality, an innocence, a spontaneity that flows from me, immersed fully in itself, whether in the form of sadness, pain, or frustration or in excitement, joy, and laughter. It is my song, my unfolding— inspired, alive, very much like the poem of life the very young child creates in his solitary encounters with the shape and feel of soft and hard, of high and low, the textures of his world, and especially the range of human faces. In his innocence, in his passion for life, the child does not see or hear the bad news that is often there before him, but rather he lives freely, deeply in touch, unaware in any shrewd, calculating, deliberate sense.

What happens to this innocence, this spirit, this passion to be alive, to vibrate with others. It becomes quickly polluted by grown-ups who, having lost their own passion for life, their own living spirit, or at least having educated it, have become limited by the expectations, demands, and judgments of others. Controlled and calculating themselves, they want to harness the child's pure, clean, creative energy. They want to make it more useful, more competent, or more productive. The tragedy is that these grown-ups know from their own experiences that creative energy dries up when restrained; it becomes cloudy and murky, it softens, weakens, stagnates, and becomes deadened; it loses its spontaneous sense of direction, its sense of being. When energy becomes standardized, it fails to satisfy, nourish, or fulfill itself. Instead of leading to a fuller life—to peak moments within oneself and with others—it dims and dwindles or it takes substitute forms that stifle and crush the person.

In the end the young person is thrown back on himself, to the source of life from within. To know something from all levels, to experience the deepest truth concerning oneself and others, it is necessary to retreat within, to engage in a process of open inquiry and meditation that will reveal one's self to oneself. Only then is the person ready to act. The awareness of one's true place in life cannot be hurried or forced. The dialogue with oneself that leads to awareness and action must come of its own. The process may be facilitated through silence and isolation in a quiet place of nature, through music, through spontaneous writing in which the whole self guides the expression, through free drawing and painting, and often through physical release—free body movement, rhythms, and dancing.

Dialogue with oneself precedes clarity of awareness, a sense of direction, and action. This book does not supply techniques on how to make choices, nor does it offer concrete steps on how to live in essential terms, because there is no formula for a full, creative life. No formula can predict the profound awakenings and discoveries that will occur in a person's inner searching. Nevertheless, inherent in loneliness as I have come to know it are guidelines to a new life. It is these guidelines or awarenesses that I wish to share in this book in the hope that they may release potentials in others and open up possibilities that will lead to authenticity, identity, and individual growth. My own experiences in loneliness have taken me into many levels of awareness and feeling—into the differences between being alone and being lonely, into the nature and value of solitude and encounter, into honesty versus truth. I have also witnessed the loneliness of children, the struggles of the person to remain an individual while developing important relationships; I have experienced the loneliness of communication and the loneliness unique to love.

The first step to awareness and action is the struggle with oneself, the battle to be. When I am in touch with myself, whatever there is is all there—the bright, radiating lights and the dark, disturbing shadows. This faith in myself, to be who I am, extends beyond me; it does not consider the other as separate but lets life flow in its own spiraling way. I think this is the only way to authentic communication, but it is only half the picture. Sometimes in my strength, the feelings and expressions of my own identity just flow. I am unaware of the faces before me, unaware that there are always poisons in the air to pollute the burgeoning expressions of life; there are always, or nearly always, barriers to overcome, restraints to the spontaneous expression of identity. There are always people who want to educate my innocence, people who want to change my unfettered feelings into sophisticated, rational expressions—people who will not let me flow, but want me moment-by-moment to know their doubts, their reservations, their anger. But, I know as I am creating myself in anguish or in ecstasy, the creation itself must flow freely like a stream flowing into the sea. I cannot create and be aware of others' reactions to my creation at the same time. The creation would never reach a point of fulfillment. When I laugh the laughter is everything there is. When I weep all of me is in the suffer- ing. My passion for beauty, for birth, for creation is every- thing in that moment. Nothing would be more restraining or destructive than to see and hear the effects of my expression while it is being created. Nothing would stop me more quickly than to gauge the reactions of others—to modulate my words or regulate my feelings when I am encountering life. Can you imagine the poet while creating his poem alter- ing his feeling or thoughts, changing his images, his style of expression, on the basis of the judgments, reactions, and evaluations of those who surround him? Can you imagine for a moment what it would mean for a composer to judge the value of his melody on the basis of its effects on others? No, in living communication—in communication which is flowing authentically, forming itself while being expressed, and be- coming increasingly fulfilled in the flow—the person is essen- tially engaged in dialogue with himself. Creative communica- tion is free, unfettered, honest to its own nature; like the wave flowing in from the sea, it is taking its course, following its path, like a stretched beam. As long as the individual main- tains a taut faith that life is actually connected, that one man's spirit is also the spirit of mankind, that that which enables me to be alive will also nourish life itself—as long as this journey of mine becomes your journey, whatever the cre- ation, it will keep growing.

This spirit of life, this trust in one being connected with other beings, this innocence that feels deeply that my tears are your sorrows, that my joy is your laughter, is strikingly present in infants and very young children as they first encounter life. In their innocence and trust, self-communication and self-expression flow outwardly to touch and awaken, to keep the faith that being alive in spirit, feeling, and creation is the essential commitment of being human.

In times of doubt and conflict there is no other way but to find a way from within. Being a self is a responsibility as well as a right. Thus the person cannot totally destroy his real self, even though this might please others and bring a gentler life. No matter how many times he is not affirmed, no matter how many times the faith is broken—something is always there within pushing forward, insisting on expression. This inward insistence creates anxiety and threatens, for all the while the outside world demands shrewdness, modulation, and regulation, the inner self is thrusting forward, requiring self-expression. If it weren't for this unique life force, we would all become robots—controlled, regulated, attuned to the rules and demands of others. Man is not a mechanical instrument who can be activated by pushing a button and he never will be. No matter how totally he is conditioned, in the strangest moments his spirit will rise again. It would be much easier if we could just get rid of ourselves, if we could once and for all kill our own spirits, and engage in dead communication so that *A* would say to *B* and *B* would follow with *C*, in a smooth logical set of reactions 1, 2, 3, 4 all leading to 5—and all predetermined, programmed, dead. But, fortunately, we cannot get rid of this spirit, we cannot kill it; and no matter how completely it has been tampered with, we have to live with it and it keeps coming back to haunt and disturb us just when we think we have everything in control.

It would be simpler if we knew our enemy, if the saboteur

would show his face; but the most effective enemy, like the most effective germ or poison, is unseen. The snake is not completely evil. More often it appears indirectly in the form of, "Yes, but—" in people who affirm with reservations, people who qualify, who dam up the stream, not all at once in one sharp rejection or rebuke, but little by little in insidious ways. And these qualifications have an impact because they come from people who have the power to stop the flow of life, to interfere, to restrain—one's lover, parents, friends, or relatives. They come from people who matter and who have the power to affect our fate and destiny. "I love you but I wish you could be more considerate of me." "You do good work but I know you could improve even more." "I like the way Steve is sitting if he would take his thumb out of his mouth." "What you say interests me but the way you say it makes me angry." And on and on it goes, so many communications that tie a person in knots unless he has strength and clarity of being, and even then it takes regular encounters with oneself, to stay in touch. So much in the world is directing us, it is difficult to keep one's unique identity alive.

It is just this staying in touch with one's own self in the face of the invasion of "love" that is essential in the battle to be. I often experience this struggle in my hours alone, and with it comes the feeling of being tampered with, of being imposed upon, and the determination to come back alive and whole. The following is an expression of self-dialogue in the aftermath of misunderstanding and broken communication:

> Something there inside, deeply lonely, in my inability to say what was in my heart. Somehow, the words, words of pain, words of shock in response to being misunderstood, tried to come but nothing made sense, nothing expressed

what was there, hidden inside—there to see, to feel, to know; what was inside remained stifled, trapped, imprisoned. How could it be otherwise? *I* was not there; my words were far removed from the lonely silence within, from the feeling of being denied, observed, looked upon. In that moment, sharing was all that mattered, communication that came from suffering and love and from the sudden breakthrough to beauty, to life, to me, and therefore to a new beginning, hungering for a true meeting after a long, long time. It was a hard journey back but it was even harder being stopped in that cold moment of incomprehension, by words that questioned, explained, analyzed. If only you could have felt something sever in me, something I had reached after a long, hard struggle. If only you could have known that what had broken was not just momentary, but a spirit and life that had come through all those uncertain, doubting, fragile times, all those endings and beginnings and then, finally, coming all the way inside, all of me, anew, joyous, firm, singing, inspired, all the way home to me and to you. You stood there detached, not knowing that it was not only my song but my soul crying in the darkness and slowly coming back into the light—free, open, totally there to meet, to know, to share. And then the life was shattered in words about objectivity, sophistication, knowledge. A clear, clean "No" would have been less painful, and more acceptable; but the in-between was more than I could take. As if questions and words and labels could ever touch the life inside, could ever know the suffering from which that creation came, the loneliness of loving and not being free to be fully myself in that love. The urgency and necessity to create a new self that included you in those experiences we still could share and value. And so it ended once more; our communication died. Would there be another time? Was there in me a new life to be born, a life of silence and of real dialogue? I could see but one way; back to my solitary self, back to my solitude, to my own dreams, to the lonely life that gave me courage and strength to live and to continue to be.

In the hours alone, it is possible to come to know oneself again, to end the confusion and depression, and begin to live again in a real way, from the wisdom of one's senses, and in the process to choose this rather than that. But while a person is struggling in lonely silence to find his way back to life again, to give birth to a new path that comes from within, to restore his spirit and passion for life, he needs strong, unqualified, affirming voices; he needs to avoid rejecting people, tentative people, and the "yes-but" people who surround him. Only the totally affirming, spontaneous, and unreserved can help him in this struggle and give him the courage and strength to return alone to his thoughts and feelings. Only they can help him discover what he really wants to do, and with whom he can take this journey. Help of this kind does not come through words of praise and approbation, but by the honest, full presence of real persons and by their respect for solitude and privacy—their willingness to let the person risk the darkness and go within alone. A dying spirit must be mourned, a broken pattern of life must be healed, the living embers of one's self must be ignited again. Then the poem that is born will come from a heart and spirit and mind that anticipates a new life, a beginning, and the words of this poem will bring a unique message if we can but hear it and let it enter our own selves in its pure form, just as it is, and move us to our own response.

A letter I wrote recently describes my struggle to remain alive after a full day of being pushed into one meeting after another, none of which had any human substance, each of

which was suddenly terminated—masses of people questioning me, talking about me as if I weren't there, addressing me
in an I-It manner, searching for justification and defense of
ideas and values, rather than listening, feeling, experiencing.
Here I was alive, humanly present, and most of the communications focused on externals, on details rather than real dialogue and encounter. The next morning I faced an audience
of about 2500 people. Suddenly I felt alienated from the
audience, the room, the entire set-up. I was experiencing a
form of psychic dying, a feeling of death in the air, the merci-
less presence of a number of people waiting for a lecture,
waiting for a polished speech, waiting to be aroused, stimulated, to be given something in finished form. I was determined to create an "address" based on my own immediate
awareness and conviction, as the following letter testifies:

> The source of my intense emotional state is, in the ulti-
> mate sense, a mystery but I know I was experiencing a
> deep sadness connected with my desire to stay in touch
> with the truth, a truth that did not have merely an idea-
> tional content but that was rooted in everything human. I
> had been living on the fringes those past few days, from
> the first moment when I met Don and saw him caught up
> in logistics and plans that were tapping his energy and life
> to that final moment Friday morning when hundreds of
> people waited before me, anticipating "Self to One" ideas
> and insights. In that moment looking to the audience, I
> realized the impossibility of reaching outward. Almost
> instantly, I felt the separateness of audience and speaker
> and the need to transcend the social structure and find the
> real person within myself and the real people "out there."
> In a sense I had a choice: to talk about "self-to-one" com-
> munication in theory and technique or to seek the immedi-

ate truth of my own inner feelings; in other words, to ad-
just to an alienated social reality or to dissolve in the normal
sense and enter into the passion of my own feelings. For
me, there was only one way. I was experiencing naïvely and
openly the real meaning of Bertrand Russell's statement:
"I'd rather be mad with the truth than sane with lies."
What I experienced was an inspired, unsought, emotional
state—intense, overt, loss of self in unfinished moments,
in repeated beginnings and endings that never fully began
and never fully ended, desires to touch and know, to stand
out, affect and be affected by. In me was an intense wish
to feel the mystery of the experience, to meet in a real way,
nonverbally, the mass of people in front of me. At the same
time, the impossibility of feeling immediate unity with
strangers struck me at once; the only thing finally that made
sense was standing out in full-life form, in naked silence.
When the impossible appears to be happening on stage, we
know better than to believe it is happening. But I knew it
was happening, that I was actually experiencing communication with myself, powerful and moving in all the agony of
broken moments, unfinished communications, and alienating
messages. I was brief and to the point and broke off before
the intensity dissipated into sympathy, concern, deliberate-
ness, explanation.

Self-to-one communication was not being conceptualized
but was being experienced. If, somehow, the people who
were present touched me, felt me, knew me, then perhaps
the essence of all authentic self-to-one communication could
be known. The feeling that remained would be in the heart
and spirit of communication, in the experience, and not in
a rational, reasonable set of ideas. In spite of what appeared
to be, I felt within me a connection with life; and having
experienced and shared that, there is now a basis for real
communication, for new thoughts, and for ways of nurtur-
ing humanness in communication, of respecting its mystery,

and of realizing the value of being with the person and trusting the silence to support and enable continued aware-ness and growth. I hope each person will infuse his own real self in his communication and keep alive the human spirit that enhances individuality and interpersonal growth.

Thiago de Mello, an exiled Brazilian poet now living in Chile, puts my experience simply:

Be it DECREED
That now what counts is the truth,
That now what counts is life
And that hand-in-hand
We will all work for what life really is.

2 | *being alone
and
being lonely*

In my travels to colleges and universities in the United States, my views on the real nature of loneliness have been severely challenged on a number of occasions. That I would deliberately seek lonely experiences was utterly incomprehensible and crazy. Given a choice, why would anyone want to withdraw and isolate himself? Why would I prefer to be alone in a time of crisis rather than be with friends or relatives? Isn't there a thin line between intense, lonely feelings of despair and the severe depression and withdrawal of the mental hospital patient? Am I not in danger of going under, of feeling the pain so deeply that I will lose myself entirely? I have been chastised in letters and in person and told that unless being lonely meant simply being alone, loneliness had no advantage or value, and that it was basically a sign of defeat and failure, a symptom of breakdown in human relations. Yet I know clearly within my own self and in my observations of others that being alone, as such, is a markedly different experience from being lonely.

For me, being alone is simply the objective reality of being without others, without company. To be alone can refer exclusively to the physical fact of being by oneself, or it can refer to a psychological fact of being, the *feeling* of being alone even in a crowd, among a group of friends, or even in a relationship with one other person. But whether one is alone by oneself, or alone with others, there is no way of knowing what aloneness actually means—in substance. When I am alone, whether physically separated or in the company of others, I am engaged in a variety of specific behaviors. I may be reliving an enjoyable incident or thinking about a recent meeting. I may be imagining and anticipating a forthcoming trip or event. I may be considering some issue or problem. I sometimes am thinking over an idea or program I am planning. I have often reexamined a situation of tension or conflict and how I might approach it next time. I may just stare at and follow lines in the pavement, the shapes and forms of clouds, the colors surrounding me, or the movement of people and things. In brief, being alone contains an infinite number of possibilities. As such, without further concrete information, the phrase does not reveal the nature of the feelings or the actuality of the moment. Although I may seek it, even hunger for it, aloneness refers to a state of being—nothing more. I do not know whether being alone is a positive or negative condition until I know what it expresses for the person involved. To be alone can be purely a cognitive or intellectual experience, and a relatively insignificant fact of life. But it can also be a crucial time in one's life, a time for meditation, writing, painting, or any activity that becomes more concentrated by the aloneness. Being alone, for me, usually means an opportunity to think, imagine, plan. I choose to be alone because I desire to be quiet for awhile to consider aspects of my life and think about possibilities for

action. Often, being alone enables me to make decisions, to
say Yes or No to requests and invitations, and to come to my
own conclusions without pressure or influence from others.
In being alone I can keep in touch with my own thinking
and know more surely that my thoughts are coming from me
and not from someone else. I can also let my creations unfold
and be what they are without the support or the comments of
others. I can be more aware of my own desires and interests
and preferences. Hopefully, I can pursue my life in a way
that will enhance my growth and lead to significant learning
based on the voices from within rather than from without. It
is usually a tranquil time of self-expression and self-renewal.
For me, being alone is a valuable state; it is a way of finding
out what is happening in my life and getting back into touch
with myself, especially when I have had too much contact
with other people and have been too centered on their lives.
But "being alone," whether in a physical or psychological
sense, is not the same experience as feeling separated from
oneself and others; it is not the intense, sharp, encompassing
feeling of being lonely. Thus the being alone that is loneliness
must be distinguished from all other ways of being alone.

Being lonely is a time of crucial significance, an entering
into an unknown search, a mystery, a unique and special moment of beauty, love, or joy, or a particular moment of pain,
despair, disillusionment, doubt, rejection. Whether in deep
joy or deep sorrow, loneliness is a timeless experience, and
at the same time a revolutionary state. In the lonely time,
there may be a longing for the radical moment to continue,
a desire that it might last forever or a desperate feeling that
it will never end. There may be the intense feeling of a breach
of faith, a broken trust, the aftermath of a shattering realization. In these profound experiences of wonder or shock, it is

not enough to say "I am alone." These words do not touch
either the positive or the negative dimensions of loneliness.
To say "I feel lonely" adds a quality to being alone, a unique,
isolated state that is unlike any other way of being alone. To
be lonely means to experience the agony of living, of being,
of dying as an isolated individual or to know the beauty and
joy and wonder of being alive in solitude. Being alone is
usually a between state, a bridge to the past or the future,
while being lonely is always an immediate, here-now engagement with life at the extremes. To be alone means to be alone
with one's self—but to be lonely means to be beside and
beyond oneself, to live intensely in the moment by creating
a new self.

In speaking of loneliness, I differentiate between *existential
loneliness,* which is a reality of being human, of being aware,
and of facing ultimate experiences of upheaval, tragedy, and
change, the intrinsic loneliness of being born, of living at the
extremes, of dying; and *the anxiety of loneliness,* which is not
true loneliness but a defense that attempts to eliminate it by
constantly seeking activity with others or by continually
keeping busy to avoid facing the crucial questions of life and
death. Existential loneliness, with many variations, expresses
itself in two basic forms: *the loneliness of solitude,* which is a
peaceful state of being alone with the ultimate mystery of
life—people, nature, the universe—the harmony and wholeness of existence; and *the loneliness of a broken life,* a life
suddenly shattered by betrayal, deceit, rejection, gross misunderstanding, pain, separation, illness, death, tragedy, and
crisis that severely alter not only one's sense of self, but the
world in which one lives, one's relationships, and work
projects.

Every real experience of loneliness involves a confrontation or an encounter with oneself. By "confrontation" I mean the direct challenge of facing a conflict, the willingness to experience fear, anger, sorrow, pain, intensely and deeply, when these feelings are caused by a sense of urgency, loss, or disillusionment. The confrontation shakes up the individual, puts him in a turbulent state, and forces him to use new energies and resources to come to terms with his life—to find a way to himself.

The "encounter," on the other hand, is a joyous experience of self-discovery, a real meeting of self-to-self. It contains an exciting flow of feeling from the union of being lonely while at the same time feeling connected with life. It includes a sense of harmony and well-being. It may be the sudden, glorious experience, "I feel joy in being me." Or it may be the silent presence of love and inner dialogue that puts the person in touch with real life and with the natural beauties of the universe. Both the encounter and the confrontation are ways of advancing life and coming alive in a relatively dead or stagnant world; they are ways of breaking out of the uniform cycles of behavior: the repetitive habits of communication and the social, filial, and professional roles and games that people play.[1]

In loneliness, some compelling, essential aspect of life is suddenly challenged, threatened, altered, denied. At such times only by entering into loneliness, by steeping oneself in the experience and allowing it to take its course and to reveal itself is there hope that one's world will achieve harmony and unity. Then the person can begin again, born as a new self, with openness, spontaneity, and trust. What I experience within myself, and what I yearn for from other persons is an

1. Clark Moustakas, "Confrontation and Encounter," in *Creativity and Conformity* (Princeton, N.J.: D. Van Nostrand Co., Inc., 1967).

acceptance and valuing, a tacit agreement to let the loneliness be, whether in solitude or in crisis. Abraham Maslow,
referring to a different kind of experience, expresses this feeling of letting it be and going all the way with it:

> No blocks against the matter-in-hand means that we let
> it flow in upon us. We let it wreak its will upon us. We let
> it have its way. We let it be itself. Perhaps we can even ap-
> prove of its being itself . . . a kind of trust in the self and a
> trust in the world which permits the temporary giving up of
> straining and striving, of volition and control, of conscious
> coping and effort. To permit oneself to be determined by the
> intrinsic nature of the matter-in-hand here-now . . .[2]

In contrast, being alone without the explicit condition of
loneliness, is an act of conscious control, volition, thought,
and determination. Being alone is a necessary pause; being
lonely is an ultimate condition. Being alone implies an evolu-
tion or continuity of experience, while being lonely means a
total, radical change. Being alone is a way back to others.
Being lonely is a way back to oneself.

2. Abraham H. Maslow, *The Farther Reaches of Human Nature* (New
York: The Viking Press, 1971), p. 67.

3 | *the lonely child*

I want to begin with the lonely child in *me*. Standing alone. Walking on the edge of darkness. Entering the night. Sitting quietly in the sunlight. I can remember, and I can feel the sense of being separate, of wanting to be separate and know me. Sometimes the only way was to escape into the woods, a woods sparsely populated with dwarfed, shaggy trees. Yet when I closed my eyes and sat silently, I could feel the wind; I could hear the chirping of the birds; and I could imagine the beauty of the forest, the mountains, and the sea. Sometimes I watched the movements of the clouds and, through my own self, created images, shapes, and forms that brought a sense of wonder into my life. In that solitude, a spirit arose, a passionate urgency to be who I am—in poetry, in dance, in story and song. It was not only my own unfolding, my own destiny that was at stake, not only my own listening to me, but it was also my awareness of misfortune—the poverty, sickness, and death in the world—and my fervor to create a truly human, full life everywhere. I wanted to laugh, to create joy, to plunge into the moment fully, to savor everything; but

25

I was also aware of how long it takes to finally make it, to
fully encounter life. I felt I would have to wait forever. I was
impatient to live now, but there were always barriers to overcome and caution on all sides.

Then somehow the exciting moment arrived and at last I
entered wanting to remain there forever. For a time I experienced the enduring nature of life and felt the timeless quality of love and its spontaneity and freedom; I felt reborn into
a real knowledge of myself and others. That was it—to have
both the serenity and the passion all at once, the discovery
and certain knowledge of my own strength and value, the
confidence in reaching out, touching, embracing, dancing
—yes, and the trust that my response of love would be
returned. But then, as now, within that innocent, total
letting-go, there was a fleeting deep-down uneasiness that
pain and suffering always follow, that in every real beginning
there is an ending. Within that free-floating confident spirit,
there also came the unsettling question—perhaps I had more
in me to put into the moment. There was so much more to
experience, and I wanted to break out into the open and fully
tap the potential. It is this awareness of life's potential—the
waiting for something to be born, reaching out and loving,
innocently, honestly, purely—and then suddenly it is gone.
It is just this impatience to enter real life again and to experience it freely that is the lonely child in me. It is just this
awareness of the passing of time, the lost potential, the unfinished moments when I don't see, or when I hold back, that
arouses the lonely adult in me.

Sometime ago I became interested in the study of alienation and loneliness especially among children in schools and
hospitals and in their families. I saw the spontaneous expres-

sions of young children change into apathy and reserve, the vigorous, spirited involvement in learning and living change into mechanical, deathlike behavior. I saw grown-ups reward and punish, sometimes with the direct use of authority and sometimes with subtle and devious methods. I saw a child's right to express his own identity and to grow as a unique person throttled by loud, demanding orders and by sweet, manipulating words. What shocked me then and shocks me still is that in spite of all the evidence that alienation poisons, reduces, and limits the self, authoritarian people continue to impose their standards and values on others; they think they should direct and control what a child learns and how he learns. Not only do these people—these parents, teachers, doctors, nurses, businessmen, lawyers—shrewdly and efficiently manage to restrain and deny freedom of choice, but they actually kill sources of life, which when unfettered and free enhance the individuality, uniqueness, and integrity of the self. The official spokesmen of our society still delude themselves with the belief that the docile submission to rules and external standards is still the best basis for human relations and for responsible living. They believe this in spite of the destruction and unhappiness that surround them, in spite of the mass murders of children and families by men who follow orders in an immoral and mechanical way.

The truth revealed itself then, and reveals itself today, that conformity to the expectations and demands of others and submissive obedience to rules and regulations are the most basic forms of alienation. Eventually self-denial and self-neglect lead to unhealthy, neurotic forms of behavior. Not only must the child submit and give up his own desires, interests, and judgments but he must do so gratefully. The child should, if he is to live a "respectable" life, participate and assist in the execution of his own self. However, the self is never totally destroyed. It has a life of its own, whether we choose to recognize it or not. Often the path a person takes to avoid being alienated from himself is the path of loneliness and solitude.

Fourteen is sometimes the loneliest age for a child. He suddenly begins to question the important connections in his life—his family, friends, and the activities he thought represented his interests. He suddenly realizes that his fantasies, daydreams, and ambitions are all games he has been playing and that have been played on him. He becomes aware that everything he considered real is not real anymore. He no longer knows the people he lives with or the places that have been important in his world; he doesn't know who he is anymore. The crisis of awakening to his aloneness and doubt is frightening, and so he withdraws deeper and deeper into himself to try to figure out what he can trust as being real, who he can trust, who he is.

This was Richard's experience when he began to distrust the people in his life. He retreated into a private world of questioning and doubting, searching for an answer to the deceit, manipulation and betrayal that surrounded him in school and in his neighborhood. He wanted to live honestly but he no longer knew where or how to begin. Within his yearning to live in a real way was the terror of unreality and death, and the silent quest to find the truth, to affirm it and to become one with it. Isolated, withdrawn, alone, his darkness increased and the fear of total dissipation of self overwhelmed him. He began to feel that nothing mattered; his body stiffened. For some days he remained in his room in an unmovable, frozen state.

Then one day a friend approached him, sat quietly nearby and waited. The suffering was his own yet Richard could also feel the human presence of someone who loved him, someone who would not interfere. Their communication was silent and wordless yet a bond began to grow between them. Slowly, painfully Richard began to weep, his tears flowed freely, his muscles awakened and for the first time in many days, he felt movement and life. His breathing deepened. He was connected with another human being in a way that he felt to be real. He had made a contact that he knew he could trust. None of the old patterns would ever be the same, the break with them was complete, but the feeling was not one of desperation or helplessness. His world was dying but in that moment of touching he felt the suffering and love of another person and he knew he could begin again. Once more he entered a solitary journey but it took him out of his room, into the sunshine, where he began to feel new energy and a desire to live again. As he healed, he made honest, real contacts with people, at first only with individual members of his family— but soon he began to reach out to others again. He began to live in accordance with his real self and this was all that mattered.

Somewhere within the person the desire to live honestly and actually is always present. This desire for life expresses itself in anxiety and general dissatisfaction, in feelings of psychic starvation, sometimes in sudden violence, and sometimes in fears and terrifying nightmares. The self can be imprisoned and caged, but as long as the person is breathing, however distorted and blunted his senses may be, some part of his song will be sung, some line of his poetry will escape, some indication of his dance will come through. Messages from his inner self will be there if we can but read them. When the outer behavior does not match the inner self, it is a huge struggle to remove the layers of dishonesty and phonyness. But the potential for real feelings to be aroused and experienced is always present. True expressions of identity threaten to come forth. At any time the person may break out, as Mary Barnes, a so-called schizophrenic, broke out in her hollow tree.

There was once a tree in the forest who felt very sad and lonely for her trunk was hollow and her head was lost in mist. Sometimes, the mist seemed so thick that her head felt divided from her trunk. To the other trees, she appeared quite strong but rather aloof, for no wind ever bent her branches to them. She felt if she bent she would break yet she grew so tired of standing straight. So it was with relief that in a mighty storm, she was thrown to the ground. The tree was split, her branches scattered, her roots torn up and her bark was charred and blackened.

She felt stunned and though her head was clear of the mist she felt her sap dry as she felt her deadness revealed when the hollow of her trunk was open to the sky. The other trees looked down and gasped and didn't know whether to turn their branches politely away or whether to try and cover her emptiness and blackness with their green and brown. The tree moaned for her own life and feared to be suffocated by theirs. She felt she wanted to lay bare, and open, to the wind and the rain and the sun, and that in time she would grow up again, full and brown from the ground. So it was, that with the wetness of the rain, she put down new roots and by the warmth of the sun she stretched forth new wood.

In the wind her branches bent to other trees and as their

leaves rustled and whispered, in the dark and in the light,
the tree felt loved and laughed with life.[1]

I met Joseph in my work in an inner-city school in Detroit.
He had often been only a few feet in front of me or beside me,
but it was three long weeks before I was actually aware of his
presence. He was one of many, many faces during my weekly
visits to an elementary school where I was working toward
humanizing learning, enriching life, and introducing art and
creative processes into the everyday experiences of children
and teachers. Joseph, small, quiet, hidden, continually sucked
his thumb. When I finally noticed him he stood out in a striking and appealing way. In time I learned that Joseph had
resigned himself to isolation and loneliness; his withdrawal
was a kind of truce, having been ignored, defeated, and
beaten regularly. Having discovered him, I was shocked that
in the next four weeks not once did another child approach
him, speak to him, or as far as I could tell, even know that he
existed—nor did Joseph ever address any of the other children in his class. His teacher spoke to him a total of three
times, and in each instance it was the same message: "Joseph,
take your thumb out of your mouth and sit up straight!"

Aware now of Joseph's loneliness, I approached him frequently, sometimes kneeling down close to him, meeting his
eyes directly, and waiting for whatever he wished to share
with me. I soon learned that Joseph's communications would
come when he was ready and not from my initiating the contacts. Although I continued to let him know I wanted to know

1. Mary Barnes, "The Hollow Tree" included in "Who Is Mad? Who Is
Sane?" by James S. Gordon, *The Atlantic Monthly*, Vol. 227 (January, 1971)
p. 66.

him, he did not respond outwardly; but inside something
must have been growing, for one day I heard a tapping on the
window of the classroom during lunch recess. I looked out
and saw Joseph standing alone, while his classmates were
busy with games in the snow. I motioned to him to come in,
but he just kept pointing at something in the room. I was so
amazed by his motioning to me that I had difficulty in focus-
ing on anything but the excitement in his face. At last I saw
that he was pointing to a large planter filled with small, green
shoots sprouting in rich, black soil. There in the center was a
large, tall plant, and Joseph was pointing to it, shyly but with
glowing eyes. We stood there for a while admiring his plant
as he continued to communicate with gestures, in pantomime,
in a real flow of feeling. He was actually smiling, and it was
sheer joy being together for the first time. We danced with
our eyes, and slowly Joseph came to trust me. He came into
the room and took my hand. I entered his world, wondering
if this was his first actual human meeting. Holding him close,
I heard his voice and the sounds of his speech thrilled me. I
felt joyously alive.

> "Are you a kid or a grown-up?" he asked.
>
> "What would you say, Joseph?"
>
> "When I see you drive your car I think you're a grown-up,
> but when you talk to me, when you play with me, I think
> you're a kid."
>
> "I see. I like that, Joseph."
>
> "My daddy never plays with me. He's always a grown-up."
>
> "What about your mom?"
>
> "I don't have a mom. She died when I was three and now
> I have a second mom. But I remember my first mom and I
> miss her."

"That must be hard. Perhaps when I come here we can play together."

Joseph held onto me silently for the remainder of the lunch recess. After this first encounter he often shared important events in his life. But, though I tried to involve him with other boys and girls in the room, he still chose to be alone.

I have been frequently startled by his awareness of what is happening in the classroom and outside. He notices the details of weather, the nature of the clouds, and the colors and makes of cars, but his spirit has been broken and his unique vitality dimmed. It is painful to hear him speak of the cruelty, denial, and rejection he experiences at home, and it is painful to see him unnoticed and ignored in school. One day recently he removed a Band-Aid from his finger to show me four places where his brother had cut him with a knife. His mother had been resting and told him not to bother her. His father, after work, had been tired and told him he did not want to hear about his troubles. Perhaps, in time, having learned to trust me, he will find others in his school and begin to create friendships; but in my dark moments I wonder if he has the resources and the strength to overcome the brutality and the callousness of his life at home. I know that Joseph is not cast out of metal. He has grown and changed. He is more often relaxed. He moves more freely, with expanded muscles and deeper, fuller breathing but he still prefers to be alone. I respect his loneliness. It seems an essential and vital part of him. I hope others will come to know him as the unique person he is and that he will be valued as someone of quality and depth. Perhaps our friendship will serve as a model through which his excitement in living and being will radiate and enable others to notice him and feel his presence. He is on good terms with himself. Perhaps one day he will be on good terms with others.

I also want to introduce you to Bill. Bill never knew what separated him from other children and grown-ups, but he clearly knew the separation existed. Somehow, he did not feel free to be who he was except when he was alone. Then his thoughts and feelings opened, and he entered life, trusting that he could go wherever his feeling and energy took him, free to question himself, free to be. But with others he felt he was being tested, watched, judged; and slowly, slowly he felt the chains beginning to bind him; he felt he was expected to be a certain kind of a child instead of the person he was. His teacher described him as retarded and as an oddball. As far as she was concerned he had nothing to offer himself or anyone else. "Here he is in third grade," she shouted at me, "and he can't even read our primer yet." "Oh yes he can," I answered quietly, "but he freezes when he's told to read something that doesn't matter to him and when he is being judged." For several weeks in my therapy with Bill he had been reading ten-syllable chemical names that I still have difficulty pronouncing. If ever a child pursued his questions it was Bill, and he pursued them until he was satisfied or until he exhausted himself and whatever resources he could locate. He conducted increasingly advanced experiments in chemistry, and he knew all the elements and many compounds. As he charted his weekly experiment, he carefully read the directions and proceeded to perform his miracles. I suggested to his teacher that she let him pursue his own interests in whatever subject he preferred to focus on, provide him with help when he requested it, and permit him to report back if he wished. She looked at me as if I had lost my mind, but she agreed to make a bargain with Bill. "Bill," she said, "you can take part of the day for things you want to do and part of it you'll do what I want you to do." Eventually, she came to respect Bill's abilities, but she never really cared for him, never gave him the feeling that he was important in her world.

Bill's mother, in our first meetings, glowingly described the charm and energy of her youngest son, but Bill—well—he bored her. He never had much to say. She had to do all the work in their conversations, and liking him—that was a struggle; enjoying him was almost impossible. "He never does what I expect him to do. He always wants to do things his way. And when he talks it's usually in monosyllables."

Wow, I thought, are we talking about the same person? In my first hour with Bill he started talking the moment he entered the room and he didn't stop talking until our time was up. I was intrigued, fascinated, speechless. He opened our session with a ten-minute lecture on ESP that excited me more than most similar lectures I have heard. He compared the capacities for psychic communication of his grandmother, his mother, and a number of his neighbors. He had observed that young children were more psychically imaginative than their parents. During the talk he covered out-of-body travel, poltergeist phenomena, precognition, and clairvoyance; he used the technical terms appropriately and related them to his own life. "I have to control my thoughts," he said, "because if I let them go, strange, mysterious things begin to happen. When I concentrate hard I see spirits in the furniture, ceiling, and walls, and once our table moved without anyone touching it." From ESP he went on to pollution, differentiating air, water, and land, talked about the chemicals that create the problem, and expressed his concern over the

future of mankind. In addition to ESP and pollution, he indicated his interest in chemistry, biology, electronics, and
magic. He talked about what it must be like to be insane and
what it must be like to be free to develop all of your potentials.

When I listed the topics Bill had discussed with me and
quoted some of his statements, his mother looked at me in
disbelief and astonishment, "Where did he learn all these
things?" she asked. "Perhaps I should stop doing all the talking and start listening." In time, Bill's mother learned to enter
his world somewhat and found it an exciting place to be, but
she never fully understood it or why Bill preferred to be in it
so much of the time rather than with other people.

I am still intrigued with Bill's attention span and his sustained way of pursuing questions. I have journeyed with him
to outer space, the depths of the ocean, the top of volcanoes,
and deep in the soil. I have studied minute lines on floors and
tabletops with him, and I have watched liquids move and ob-
jects change their directions. He remained fully alive as long
as I didn't try to steer his course.

Perhaps he will always be somewhat restrained in the presence of others. Perhaps others will always find him a strange
person who is difficult to accept in his autonomy and independence. When he is alone he can think his own thoughts
and pursue them to their natural end. Others are now trying
to make his talents useful and exploit his abilities. He is difficult to classify and pigeon-hole, but then, as he put it, "That's
their problem, not mine." Bill's values are internal, they are
not worn on the surface where everyone can see. His spirit is
strong and undeniable. I feel certain he will remain a lonely
person, but he will continue to find his place in the world in
spite of what others may try to do to him.

4 | *loneliness*
and
solitude

To remain in touch with oneself as an individual requires an awareness of the conditions in society that threaten to chain man to a life of security and comfort, to a life of habit and routine, where feelings are modulated and disguised. Once a fixed pattern of living is established, the person only dimly perceives his own inner response to experience, his own real thoughts and feelings. He only vaguely notices that increasing regularity exacts a penalty of monotony and dullness and that organization and efficiency often lead to boredom. When one really looks, one sees the same faces and voices, the same pathways, the same motions and actions, appearing and reappearing. The routine nature of existence may not be recognized, but the alarm clock puts modern man into motion in the morning and into bed at night, and the same old roads are being traveled.

As long as habit and routine dictate the pattern of living, new dimensions of the self will not emerge; new interests will not develop. The human scene becomes one of still life, where familiar images become commonplace and words and gestures repeat a well-known refrain. In such a state, it takes a sudden jolt to shock the person into an awareness that his existence is basically mechanical and dead. It often takes a severe threat to make one aware of one's failure to be, of one's failure to discover new meaning and value in living. The sudden recognition that daily life has become petrified in order to achieve security and to establish a steady, stable existence may produce severe anxiety. When the person is alone and considers the real nature of his existence, when he becomes aware of the emptiness of his life, he stands mute before himself. He discovers what really matters in giving new meanings and directions to his life. In solitude, the person often reaches almost wordless states of experience and a vividness of inner life in aesthetic and spiritual forms. Here is an example of an experience of solitude in nature that a student recently shared with me:

> While watching a sunset during a vesper service, I discovered the peace and tranquility of nature. The sun slipped behind the distant mountain tops as I watched, enraptured. The mystical murmurings of the trees added a ghostly quality to the gentle sound of singing which flowed lazily toward me on the wings of the wind. In the valley everything seemed serene and carefree. A chipmunk scurried across a rock and birds called soothing messages to their mates. I could not bear to shatter the sacred silence of the sky or to veil the sounds of nature behind those of man. I sat silently watching the ancient ritual of the wild as the world prepared for nightfall with its slumber and rest.

Solitude is a return to one's own self when the world has grown cold and meaningless, when life has become filled with people and too much of a response to others. Solitude is as much an intrinsic desire in man as his gregariousness. Hermits, solitary thinkers, independent spirits, recluses, although often stigmatized in the modern world, are healthy expressions of man's dialogue with himself. The overdevelopment of socialized man, the constant need for involvement with people, is often motivated by a fear of discovering one's own real self and by the anxiety of remaining stagnant in the presence of surrounding life. Socialized man too often lacks the courage to become more profoundly aware, to stretch his resources to new levels, and to participate in the mystery of living, which is ineffable, indescribable, unpredictable, and, in some ways, private and unsharable. The response to others, however meaningful or meaningless, can be broken only through solitude. It is unlike any other experience—not to have to respond to others, not to be stimulated or challenged by others, just to be alone.

In solitude man does not deal with concrete and practical realities, for being practical is simply another way of socializing, of submitting or disclosing one's secrets in material ways, of giving statements that can be counted, explained, and analyzed. The truly solitary process is not tangible and materialistic; it cannot be defined and quantified. It remains aesthetic and mystical. The moment it is studied and "understood" it becomes something else, something radically unlike the original solitude, with all its vague, diffuse visions and dreams, with all its imagining and wondering and its incomprehensible powers that sensitize and cleanse. In the process the individual often purges himself of false idols, distortions, and deceptions; he creates a new picture of reality and reaches for the truth. The moment of solitude is a spontane-

ous, awakening experience, a coming to life in one's own way,
a path to authenticity and self-renewal.

An example of solitude in facing the problem of separation
and death is Lara's visit to the funeral home for the final encounter with Doctor Zhivago. Here we see the significance
of self-reflection, meditation, and dialogue, the continuity of
life in the face of death, of ongoing meaning in the presence
of an apparent end of a relationship, of self-confrontation and
struggle and determination to keep on living and growing, to
keep on loving and valuing in a relationship—more than this,
to find new awareness and meaning.

In this autobiographical moment, Lara has just entered the
room where Doctor Zhivago's body is displayed for mourning
friends and relatives. People pour into the room to offer respect and tribute to the dead man. But Lara is really not
aware of anyone else; she does not hear the voices or the painful sobs, nor does she see the grief-stricken, mourning faces;
she does not hear the shuffling of the crowd, the coughs of the
men, or the cries of the women. She is alone with herself—
the beating of her heart, the images and reveries of rich moments once shared and reflections on the future that involve,
too, the carrying forward of her love for Yurii and the values
and dreams she shares with him. She reaches, temporarily,
the very bottom of her misery, but at the same time there is a
feeling in this room with Yurii of life being lived, of love
being experienced in all its joy and sadness. She is enveloped
momentarily in the air of a freedom and unconcern that
emanates from him, and something incomprehensible is happening to her; she is breaking free into the open, with Yurii's
help, out of sorrows that imprison her and into the joy of
liberation. Sequences of ideas, insights, truths, feelings drift

and sail freely through her, like clouds in the sky—rich dialogue and a spontaneous understanding that is warm, instinctive, immediate. In Pasternak's words:

> Oh, what a love it was, utterly free, unique, like nothing else on earth! Their thoughts were like other people's songs.
> They loved each other, not driven by necessity, by the "blaze of passion" often falsely ascribed to love. They loved each other because everything around them willed it, the trees and the clouds and the sky over their heads and the earth under their feet. Perhaps their surrounding world, the strangers they met in the street, the wide expanses they saw on their walks, the rooms in which they lived or met, took more delight in their love than they themselves did.
> Ah, that was just what had united them and had made them so akin! Never, never, even in their moments of richest and wildest happiness, were they unaware of a sublime joy in the total design of the universe, a feeling that they themselves were a part of that whole, an element in the beauty of the cosmos.
> This unity with the whole was the breath of life to them. And the elevation of man above the rest of nature, the modern coddling and worshipping of man, never appealed to them. A social system based on such a false premise, as well as its political application, struck them as pathetically amateurish and made no sense to them.
> And now she took her leave of him, addressing him in the direct language of everyday life. Her speech, though lively and informal, was not down-to-earth. Like the choruses and monologues of ancient tragedies, like the language of poetry or music, or any other conventional mode of expression, its logic was not rational but emotional. The rhetorical strain in her effortless, spontaneous talk came from her grief. Her simple, unsolemn words were drenched in tears.

It was these tears that seemed to hold her words together
in a tender, quick whispering like the rustling of silky
leaves in a warm, windy rain.[1]

When solitude is scheduled into life, with appropriate
places and methods, its meaning and essence will be destroyed. For solitude is an art form not just for seers and for
professional seekers of truth. It comes and goes in its own
valid moments as a capacity of man that is self-initiated.

In real solitude we are expansive, limitless, free. We do not
disguise our feelings from ourselves, but rather we renew
contact with ourselves and discover who we are. At other
times we are pulled into the collective stream that surrounds
us. We experience the collective sense that we have incorpo-
rated in order to achieve recognition, security, and comfort.
In solitude, one breaks through the dead, static patterns and
has an opportunity to see life as it really is and to become
aware of a desire for new meaning, excitement, and vitality,
of a desire to be whole and to live more fully and completely.

Important as it is, at times, solitude is not enough to break
new ground, to challenge the mechanical nature of existence,
to confront life with a new reality, or to come to grips with
the pain of isolation, rejection, and death. Solitude contributes to awareness and change; it creates the setting or
climate, but often it does not carry out the theme. Dissatisfaction with life and awareness of new possibilities are sometimes not enough to create a new world. Often it is necessary
that the person feel the anguish of loneliness, that he feel cut
off from the sources of genuine life, that he feel the agony
of loss of human meaning, and that he know the tragic sepa-

1. Boris Pasternak, *Doctor Zhivago* (New York: New American Library,
1960), p. 417.

ration from his own self. It is important that the person feel the emptiness of existence all the way, in the depths of his being, and know that his deadness of spirit may be more related to his failure to live honestly than to outside pressure and defeat. It is important, too, that the individual recognize the basic loneliness of individuality, the basic loneliness of separateness, and let these feelings stand.

Loneliness and solitude are sometimes used as synonyms. According to Webster's Third New International Dictionary, loneliness means without company, solitary, not frequented by human beings, alone. From the same source, solitude is defined as a state of being alone, remote from society, lonely. While I do not believe that meaning is derived by defining terms in this way, it is important to recognize that loneliness and solitude are different though closely related experiences.

I prefer to consider loneliness and solitude in terms of the kinds of experiences that arouse these feelings. Loneliness is often evoked through experiences of rejection and feelings of guilt for not being who one is and for not actualizing one's potentialities; it occurs in the presence of tragedy, illness, and death; it is associated with a new truth that suddenly shatters old perceptions or ideas; it is connected with feeling different from other members of a group or feeling misunderstood and apart from others, with a sense of not belonging. It is frequently associated with broken relationships and separation experiences. There are many, many kinds of loneliness, but each experience is unique and each represents a different moment of life.

Here are some examples. First, Margarethe Wiest's poem of the loneliness of feeling accepted and loved for the first time:

Like birds in winter
You fed me;
Knowing the ground was frozen,
Knowing
I should never come to your hand,
Knowing
You did not need my gratitude.

Softly,
Like snow falling on snow,
Softly, so not to frighten me,
Softly
You threw your crumbs on the ground
and walked away,
Waiting.

The loneliness of death and its culmination in an experience of solitude are expressed in this letter from a friend:

All the vivid details of my experience of loneliness are still with me as if it had happened only yesterday. There was a long-distance call for me. My heart sank.

This was a loneliness I had never known before—the telephone booth closed in on me and it was almost as if I weren't breathing at all. *It was all so final!* I would never see my friend again. Religion at that moment was not enough to help me. I simply wept and wept and let go completely.

I don't remember how I spent Saturday. On Easter Sunday I attended church in a strange city, but the minister seemed to have something to say to me. I felt better, but still lonely. All this time I was fortunate enough to be traveling with another very good friend. Though I was not alone, I was lonely. It was a most unusual day, and unforgettable.

There were flowering shrubs, bright new grass, red-bricked and white-pillared colonial buildings of Hanover College in stark relief against the threatening dark sky; the sunshine made all things brighter and sharply outlined in contrast. Billowing white clouds were moving fast, piling up high against slate ones with the rays of the sun breaking through intermittently. It was one of those hot, humid days when delicate odors were more noticeable, bird notes more clear—the freshness and newness of life was all around me —it was breathtakingly beautiful. I felt momentarily one with God and my friend; I was no longer lonely. The Easter message was for me, too, and I felt I really understood somehow the truer meaning of life in death.

Then, as if all this beauty were not enough, I found a double rainbow for an anticlimax. The heavens had opened and the rain had drenched the earth. When the sun came again I followed the bands of brilliant color clear across the sky into the ground below me where the wide expanses of the Ohio River rolled brown with the muds of spring. The unreal, brightly reflected light made that part of the valley where fields were already tilled and planted a lasting painting for my mind's eye. One of the loneliest moments of my life I found the most beautiful, meaningful, and haunting I have ever experienced. I remember this feeling in an inexplainable way—sadness and longing mingled with an appreciation and awareness of beauty and a depth of emotion which was rare and inspiring.

There are times now when a lovely sunset, the scent of clover or sweet grass in June, a scarlet tanager in the tip of a tamarack, hoar frost in full moonlight in January in the quiet north woods, great symphonic music, a hermit thrush in the silence and fragrance of dusk in the jack pine plains, an unguarded expression on a loved one's face, a loon frantically calling in the mist of the early morning—these things once shared with those I love—fleetingly give me that feeling of what I call loneliness. I believe that whenever any

experience is too beautiful to phrase into words, I feel loneliness.

The loneliness of being rejected is portrayed in the following theme written by a tenth-grade boy.

> Loneliness is a depressing state of mind that none desires
> but we all endure. When I'm lonely it's not because of
> being shut away from human beings physically but when
> I'm rejected by those I respect and love. If a close friend
> turns against me I feel hurt and lonely. When I feel like a
> square block in a round hole, it brings on a form of loneli-
> ness. Sometimes my parents seem unfair; there is no one to
> turn to and I feel desolate, lost. Loneliness comes every day.
> When someone makes a thoughtless criticism that attacks
> one of my weaknesses, it takes the wind out of my sails. I
> wonder if what they say is really true. I get a small feeling
> and that's a kind of loneliness.
>
> Then there is another kind of loneliness—the kind to be
> desired. When I experience something new and wonderful,
> a new thrill, I like to be alone where I can think it over,
> remember every part of it. I like to bathe in those happy
> memories. That's a satisfying loneliness. Whether I'm in a
> happy, gratified or desolate, depressed state of mind, lone-
> liness is an important facet of my life.

The loneliness of separation is perceived as a negative experience in the following essay of a tenth-grade girl:

> Loneliness gives me a cold feeling like the loneliness the
> earth feels in winter when the birds and flowers have left
> her, and I feel as though I don't have a friend in the world.
> The whole house is lifeless now and that makes me feel
> depressed. Depression is truly a part of this feeling of lone-
> liness. It has no joy or excitement in it as houses blessed

with a happy and loving family usually do. There never seems to be anything to do. It all seems to be done, it is as if you were trapped in a strange world of loneliness, a world in which you are caught up in a great vacuum of emptiness.

A related kind of separation experience is expressed by Donna Turley in this longing for a return of intimate social relations and friendships once known, in this desire for love that cannot be.

> That deep and abiding longing I so often of late find harboring within myself . . . is now moving near the heart of me again . . . and while I listen hard enough to hear the most distant sound, it is a mellow and a mournful and a sad melody . . . a profound hurting . . . a painful coming to newness.
>
> Faint sounds of those I love are intermingled with tones that remind me of the somberest moments of my life. Oh! there's so much, so very much lost love . . . so far and wide has my caring been thrown . . . so seldom to take root and truly grow. And there's even a mournfulness in the places where it has grown most strongly and flowered most beautifully . . .
>
> I somehow want to still be holding those seeds in the palm of my hand . . . though they could never have taken root and grown into relationship and meaning had I not let them go . . . but now I cannot ever retrieve them.[2]

Paul Tillich believed that two words were created in the English language to express the two sides of man's aloneness —"loneliness" to express pain in being alone and "solitude" to express the glory of being alone. As Tillich saw it, loneliness is most widespread when we are left alone through separation

2. Donna Lee Turley, *Mosaic of My Self* (Cambridge, Mass.: Howard Doyle Publishing Co., 1968), p. 8.

or death, but it also occurs in those moments when the person
feels absolutely isolated or misunderstood or when he remains
silent and withdrawn though surrounded by people he loves.
There is also the loneliness of disappointed love or rejected
love; and, finally, there is the loneliness of guilt (the failure
to be one's real self) and the loneliness of having to die, of
anticipating death in the actual day or hour of our dying.

Solitude takes other forms: the desire toward the silence of
nature—we speak without voice to the trees and the clouds
and the waves of the sea—or the solitude of listening to
poetry, or reading it, or listening to music, or viewing works
of art. At such times we are alone even in the midst of crowds,
but we are not lonely. Silence is an essential part of solitude;
in silence there is a self-conscious, careful perceiving within,
unlike any other reality, deep and pervasive, leaving its own
distinctive mark. The real silence, says Maeterlinck, surrounds
us on every side and is the source of the undercurrents of life.
What is the innermost nature of solitude? Tillich answers as
follows: "The presence of the eternal upon the crowded roads
of the temporal. It is the experience of being alone but not
lonely . . . to face the eternal, to find others, to see ourselves." Although Tillich believed one can overcome loneliness through solitude, he saw this only as a temporary condition; inevitably, loneliness returns in the face of boredom,
emptiness, rejection, separation, illness, and death, even in
the face of love. For love itself can be lonely—more than that,
it may even intensify the sense of loneliness, as it did for
Rufus and his father in *A Death in the Family*. Here loneliness
and solitude mingle together to deepen and extend individuality and the sense of community. Rufus and his father share
an evening walk, quietly, slowly, anticipating the event, sa-
voring it and finding a strange tranquility in it. They sit on a

rock, each experiencing a kind of contentment unlike any other he has known. Rufus, in this quiet place, suddenly understands his father; he realizes that, although his father loves their home and all of them, he is more lonely than this family love can help; the love of his family increases his loneliness and makes it hard for him not to be lonely; but on the rock he feels completely himself and is on good terms with his loneliness. An important part of this feeling of love and communion between Rufus and his father comes from their being together away from home, sharing together moments of solitude and meditation, very quietly, in the dark, listening to the leaves and looking at the stars. Agee puts it this way:

> These realizations moved clearly through the senses, the memory, the feelings, the mere feeling of the place they paused at, about a quarter of a mile from home, on a rock under a stray tree that had grown in the city, their feet on undomesticated clay . . . above them, the trembling lanterns of the universe, seeming so near, so intimate, that when air stirred the leaves and their hair, it seemed to be breathing, the whispering of the stars. Sometimes on these evenings his father would hum a little and the humming would break open into a word or two, but he never finished even a part of a tune, for silence was even more pleasurable. . . . Rufus felt his father's hand settle, without groping or clumsiness, on the top of his bare head; it took his forehead and smoothed it, and pushed the hair backward from his forehead, and held the back of his head while Rufus pressed his head backward against the firm hand, and, in reply to that pressure, clasped over his right ear and cheek, over the whole side of the head, and drew Rufus' head quietly and strongly against the sharp cloth that covered his father's body, through which Rufus could feel the breathing ribs; then relinquished him. . . . he saw that his father's eyes

had become still more clear and grave and that the deep
lines around his mouth were satisfied; and looked up at what
his father was so steadily looking at, at the leaves which
silently breathed and at the stars which beat like hearts. He
heard a long, deep sigh break from his father, and then his
father's abrupt voice: "Well . . ." and the hand lifted from
him and they both stood up. The rest of the way home they
did not speak, or put on their hats.[3]

In contrast to the powerful experience of being lonely,
even in the presence of gentler forces, solitude contains basically tranquil tones and themes and ineluctable feelings of
dreams and memories, of desires and imaginings. In solitude
there is peace and joy and a sense of the eternal rhythms of
life, a natural beauty that grows and expands, quietly, like
the peaceful movements of a stream, then suddenly the person is in touch with life and the mystery in the universe. This
is the experience of the central character in *Green Mansions*.
Temporarily isolated in a forest in the Quenevata Mountains,
he comes upon a single white flower that he has never seen
before, and the exquisite moment in nature comes to life.

After I had looked long at it, and passed on, the image
of that perfect flower remained so persistently in my mind
that on the following day I went again, in the hope of seeing it still untouched by decay. There was no change; and
on this occasion I spent a much longer time looking at it,
admiring the marvelous beauty of its form, which seemed
so greatly to exceed that of all other flowers . . . cut by a
divinely inspired artist from some unknown precious stone,
of the size of a large orange and whiter than milk, and yet,
in spite of its opacity, with a crystalline luster on the sur-

3. James Agee, *A Death in the Family* (New York: Avon Books, 1959),
pp. 23–24.

face. Next day I went again, scarcely hoping to find it still unwithered; it was fresh as if only just opened; and after that I went often, sometimes at intervals of several days, and still no faintest sign of any change, the clear, exquisite lines still undimmed, the purity and luster as I had first seen it. . . . it would continue to bloom when I had looked my last on it; wind and rain and sunlight would never stain, never tinge, its sacred purity; the savage Indian, though he sees little to admire in a flower, yet seeing this one would veil his face and turn back; even the browsing beast crashing his way through the forest, struck with its strange glory, would swerve aside and pass on without harming it.[4]

Here we see two functions of solitude: the awakening of the incomprehensible, the essential mystery of human existence, and the birth of the inexplicable within ourselves. From these dimensions of self coming to life, we experience a sense of wonder, an awareness that casts freshness and light, an expansiveness of self, perceiving vividly and clearly. Hermann Hesse, a truly lonely figure in modern literature, believed that self-awareness could be achieved only through solitude and self-reflection. In *Demian,* he wrote:

Few people nowadays know what man is. Many sense this ignorance and die the more easily because of it. . . . I do not consider myself less ignorant than most people. I have been and still am a seeker, but I have ceased to question stars and books; I have begun to listen to the teachings my blood whispers to me. My story is not a pleasant one; it is neither sweet nor harmonious as invented stories are; it has the taste of nonsense and chaos, of madness and dreams—like the lives of all men who stop deceiving themselves.

4. W. H. Hudson, *Green Mansions* (New York: Random House, 1944), pp. 225–26.

Each man's life represents a road toward himself, an attempt at such a road, the intimation of a path. No man has ever been entirely and completely himself. Yet each one strives to become that—one in an awkward, the other in a more intelligent way, each as best he can. . . . Some never become human, remaining frog, lizard, ant. Some are human above the waist, fish below. Each represents a gamble on the part of nature in creation of the human. We all share the same origin, our mothers; all of us come in at the same door. But each of us—experiments of the depths— strives toward his own destiny. We can understand one another; but each of us is able to interpret himself to himself alone.[5]

Solitude and loneliness are not easy paths to take, because inevitably they challenge the stable pattern of existence, and, in the process, questions and doubts are raised about the meaning and the reality of life. In these moments the individual questions the genuineness, the validity of his own existence. Disenchantment with routine, sudden awareness of the emptiness of life rise up in moods of restlessness and boredom. Sometimes man escapes monotony and routine through drugs or alcoholism, but when he takes the direct path to himself and stays on this path he inevitably experiences loneliness and solitude. Hesse puts the matter even more emphatically:

Each man had only one genuine vocation—to find the way to himself. He might end up as poet or madman, as prophet or criminal—that was not his affair, ultimately it was of no concern. His task was to discover his own destiny —not an arbitrary one—and live it out wholly and resolutely within himself. Everything else was only a would-be exist-

5. Hermann Hesse, *Demian* (New York: Harper & Row, Publishers, 1965), Prologue.

ence, an attempt at evasion, a flight back to the ideals of the masses, conformity and fear of one's own inwardness. The new vision rose up before me, glimpsed a hundred times, possibly even expressed before but now experienced for the first time by me. I was an experiment on the part of Nature, a gamble within the unknown, perhaps for a new purpose, perhaps for nothing, and my only task was to allow this game on the part of primeval depths to take its course, to feel its will within me and make it wholly mine. That or nothing! [6]

Man strives for new directions; he seeks to find vitality and excitement, and as he does he awakens to new images; the old patterns and bonds are broken. Then the individual is cut off from what he knows, from the ordinary ways of life, and, standing off by himself, looking within, he questions the reality of what he has been perceiving and valuing. I have had many experiences in which I entered into my private thoughts in search of new truth and meaning. In such moments, human distance is real, and a lonely figure waits and searches for a light that is not an illusion and a path that will not turn out to be just one more fantasy. I want to know that the step I take is real, that my heartbeat is its own, that my words belong to me, that my ideals have a place in reality. I want to feel my anguish and pain and know that love will not be shattered, that my dreams will survive the moments of doubt and terror. But, at times, life is empty and meaningless and ugly and terribly, terribly denying and isolating. I walk for hours, talking to myself, trying to make sense out of the senselessness and shock. Then I find an isolated spot, I sit under a tree, and waves of feeling assault me, cover me intensely, until I am shattered and my mind is empty of all thought. I wait,

6. *Ibid.*, p. 108.

mindlessly, for some new hope to emerge, for some sign in the universe to make a new beginning. In a trance, I remain simply present, rooted in nature, and, by some very gradual, mysterious process, I return to a consciousness of my own existence. "Does the way I live really matter?"

To ask the question, to inquire into life, to doubt the sensibility of existence, these are not questions of a disturbed and thwarted mind. These are questions that man will always ask, in sickness and in health, because they are rooted in the organic pattern of life itself. And, because man strives for the infinite, man will forever be frustrated and discouraged, forever doomed to suffer. But in the suffering, in the struggle, in his loneliness and solitude, he achieves his individuality and his identity. When there is a striking failure in life, man will always return to himself, for, ultimately, man is alone. There is no other road but to one's own self, no other meaning but an inner reality awakened in the quiet, desperate hours when one faces the truth, when one is suddenly unbalanced and dizzy from alienation, shame, and hypocrisy. There is no other source of strength but that which exists within the regions of the self and in the mysterious powers of the universe, when one has known the sharp pain of words and feelings used as weapons or the failure of love to create a bridge of meaning between persons. There is no other life but that of the solitary, single self and a knowing that in the lonely hours the return to one's self brings with it a readiness to return to others.

references

AGEE, JAMES. *A Death in the Family.* New York: Grosset & Dunlap, Inc., 1959.

HESSE, HERMANN. *Demian*. New York: Harper & Row, Publishers, 1965.

HUDSON, W. H. *Green Mansions*. New York: Random House, 1944.

MAETERLINCK, MAURICE. *The Inner Beauty*. London: A. L. Humphreys, 1910.

MOUSTAKAS, CLARK. *Creativity and Conformity*. Princeton, N. J.: D. Van Nostrand Co., 1967.

———. *Loneliness*. Englewood Cliffs, N.J.: Prentice-Hall, Inc., 1961.

PASTERNAK, BORIS. *Dr. Zhivago*. New York: Pantheon Books, Inc., 1958.

TILLICH, PAUL. *The Eternal Now*. New York: Charles Scribner's Sons, 1963.

TURLEY, DONNA. *Mosaic of My Self*. Cambridge, Mass.: Howard A. Doyle Publishing Co., 1968.

5

*loneliness
and
encounter*

I wish to discuss ways in which the individual communicates significant dimensions of himself in relationship to one other person and in groups, and to convey the nature of loneliness in the struggle to encounter others authentically.[1]

Just as one cannot ultimately know himself through the diagnoses and definitions of others, one cannot know another person ultimately except by being there in the life of the other, listening, perceiving, waiting for significant aspects of the other person to be expressed and unfold. Steeping oneself in the world of the other and letting one's perceptions take root directly from the expressions of the other are ways of knowing the person as he is.

In the interhuman realm, the word "truth" means that men communicate directly who they are. This does not require that the one convey to the other everything that occurs to him, but only that no seeming, no facade, creep in between the one person and the other. It does not depend on one let-

1. Sections of this chapter are reprinted by permission from *Individuality and Encounter,* by Clark Moustakas (Cambridge, Mass.: Howard A. Doyle Publishing Co., 1968).

ting oneself go before another, but on the one person granting the other a share in his being. Where authenticity of the
interhuman is not found, the human element itself has been
violated. Something essential is lacking—a sense of mutuality,
a real communication of person to person. This can be
achieved in no other way but through the genuine presence
of one individual to the other. In *The Mystery of Being*, Marcel comments: "When somebody's presence does really make
itself felt, it can refresh my inner being; it reveals me to myself, it makes me more fully myself than I should be if I were
not exposed to its impact." In *Between Man and Man*, Buber
emphasizes the person-to-person value even more strongly:

> The fundamental fact of human existence is neither the
> individual as such nor the aggregate as such. Each, con-
> sidered by itself, is a mighty abstraction. The individual is
> a fact of existence in so far as he steps into a living relation
> with other individuals. The aggregate is a fact of existence
> in so far as it is built up of living units of relation. The
> fundamental fact of human existence is man with man. What
> is peculiarly characteristic of the human world is above all
> that something takes place between one being and another
> the like of which can be found nowhere in nature.[2]

Growth in a relationship is sometimes a complicated process of personal interaction, requiring an awakening to the
forces within and an awareness of subtle nuances outside, in
the words and ways of other people. The most inauthentic
person can talk about the value of being authentic and can
modulate his behavior to meet this external value. If authenticity is the rewarded attribute, the behavior of authenticity

2. Martin Buber, *Between Man and Man*, trans. Ronald Gregor Smith
(Boston: Beacon Press, 1955), pp. 202–3.

can be copied and carefully developed. But authenticity itself cannot be imitated, for it refers to the real perceptions and real feelings of the individual, not to calculated gestures, motions, and external behavior. It refers to meanings, not to words, to actualities, not to labels.

Being authentic is often a painful experience, because, along with joyful and peaceful moments, authenticity inevitably leads to conflict, anger, and dissension. In my own classes, I have known the struggle involved in remaining genuine, true to my own self, while at the same time understanding and respecting the feelings of other persons. I have attempted to keep in touch with my own thoughts and convictions, to express what I believe to be true, while at the same time wanting to know the reality of the other person's perceptions and encouraging the other person to speak openly for himself. Not long ago, the impact of authentic confrontation was clearly felt in one of my groups. On this day I had come to share an exciting discovery, for me a moment of revelation and truth. From deep regions of myself, I spoke of the meaning of beauty, faith, and love, of the ultimate values that exist in every fundamental relationship and the belief that these values can be evoked, no matter how defeated or disillusioned a person may be. Somehow I felt particularly alive and filled with the desire to awaken in my students a thirst for inquiry and experience and a hunger for companionship and communion. But I was in one world and some of my students were in another. Jim remarked that I was engaging in speculation and fantasy. He made a series of nihilistic declarations, spoken softly and quietly and even with a gentle touch. In the process I felt myself being washed away in his declarative sentences. As he talked I felt a rising anger. "What's the matter?" I asked. "When were you burned to have such sour perceptions of human beings?" He told me he knew all about canned authenticity because he was often surrounded by it. As I interpreted his fallout, it had nothing to do with authenticity but was simply another form of alienation. Surely, I thought, he knew the difference between wearing a mask of honesty and being honest, between using words of authenticity and one's own real voice. Was he doubting my authenticity, or simply taking me into his meetings with others and showing me how the keen, shrewd eye for the weaknesses of people works, the eye trained not to see the truth but to look for underlying distortions? For me, he was exhibiting a facility for uncovering the meanness, hypocrisy, and cunning of others. I felt I was being put on by a cynical stance that, in itself, did much to create distrust and to arouse suspicion and guardedness. So I told him, in direct and pointed words, that his cynism was, in itself, a reality that affected the situations he observed. He looked stunned and for several minutes simply stared blankly into space. Then, with a painful edge in his voice, he told me that I was not meeting him where he was at the moment, that my words were sharp and rejecting. He paused and added, "What you say of my cynicism is true, but you make it sound as if that's all there is to me!"

To remain silent in the issue would simply initiate a pattern of pretense between us and begin to turn our meetings into clever games. As I saw it, Jim was making the beautiful into something ugly. But was it evil to speak of it? There was something in the soft-spoken, gentle way in which he expressed himself which irritated me, particularly when he was processing my words, altering them just slightly but overturning my meanings and making them appear as mere substitutes, which could be as readily simulated and exploited as any other meanings. But as he saw it, he was simply more in touch with reality. I could not meet him in that reality without denying my own self. I could not accept what felt like a twisting of my values into current coin of knowledge. I felt that, to maintain my own identity, I had to come up against him, openly and clearly, and let him feel my indignation at being misunderstood, at being received so shrewdly. I felt I had to let him know that he was turning me off with his more sophisticated experience. So I met him, true to my own experience of the moment; he felt the sting of my words. He said I was not accepting him as he was, that I was not accepting his perceptions. But to accept him, I would have had to be dishonest with myself; I would have had to be receptive to a view of life and people that offered no constructive plan of action. My choice was between standing by him or by my own self; I could not confirm him in this conflict without violating myself.

After the strong current of feeling was expressed on both sides, we really began to listen to one another, each with his own voice, each with the integrity of his own experience. It was the first time we had met in conflict, and suddenly I realized that, until this encounter, we had never really known one another. Painful as it was, the experience had the ring of truth, the ring of something real. In the process of confrontation, neither of us wavered in his concern for honesty; each remained true to his own sights and senses. Within the anguish of anger and pain we came through this meeting to a new awareness of each other; a feeling of mutual appreciation and respect was ultimately achieved. In spite of the misunderstanding and confusion, nowhere between us was there a censoring voice. This quality of openness in conflict, of staying with a reality of life as we perceived it, made our confrontation alive with meaning. It is just this kind of vital issue that the authentic person faces, for to tell the truth about one's own self, to share with others one's real beliefs and interests and dreams, is to risk oneself, to put oneself in a vulnerable position for attack. When one shares the inner regions of himself, when one reveals his deepest feelings, convictions, and experiences, he is actually trusting others; he is offering true and vital dimensions of himself. And he remains unfinished when he is not heard; he remains unfinished when he is not received. To restore this unity of self with others, an open battle is sometimes essential. Ortega y Gasset remarks: "To be open to the other is a passive thing. What is necessary is that, on the basis of an opening, I shall act on him and he shall respond or reciprocate to me. . . . The form 'we live' very well expresses this new reality, the relation 'we'—*unus et alter*, I and the other together do something and in doing it we are."

The reality of human relations, the private worlds in which each of us lives, the singular response of our own senses, the strength of our ideas and feelings mean that often we will not be in the world of the person who is sharing and creating himself with us; we will not immerse ourselves in that person's perceptions and enable him to move forward and beyond his present being; rather, we are affected in such a way that we can only respond in opposition to the other, consistent with our own selves. When we are in conflict with others, we may withdraw into sleepy states of boredom and indifference, or we may face the person in encounter. Both acceptance and confrontation are authentic ways, because they keep the persons together in reality, and as long as they remain together, whether harmoniously or antagonistically, genuine life continues; real facets of uniqueness and individuality are present, and the real identities of the persons are emerging. Thus, both conflict and affirmation can be forms of human caring, forms of trust, and ways in which the authentic person registers his existence in the world.

In the authentic relationship, each person stands by his own perceptions. The reality of these perceptions may be expressed through silent presence and affirmation; that is, through receiving the other person as he is, listening with one's total self, and responding with appreciation and regard, thus enabling the person to feel human presence and concern and to become aware of himself. Growth of the self requires meetings between I and Thou, in which each person recognizes the other as he is; each says what he means and means what he says; each values and contributes to the unfolding of the other without imposing or manipulating. And this always means some degree of distance and independence. It does not depend on one revealing to another everything that exists within, but requires only that the person be who he is, genuinely present. Buber expresses this value in the following passage from *The Knowledge of Man*:

> When two men inform one another of their basically different views about an object, each aiming to convince the other of the rightness of his own way of looking at the matter, everything depends so far as human life is concerned, on whether each thinks of the other as the one he is, whether each, that is, with all his desire to influence the other, nevertheless unreservedly accepts and confirms him in his being this man and in his being made in this particular way. The strictness and depth of human individuation, the elemental otherness of the other, is then not merely noted as the necessary starting point, but is affirmed from the one being to the other. The desire to influence the other then does

not mean the effort to change the other, to inject one's own "rightness" into him; but it means the effort to let that which is recognized as right, as just, as true (and for that very reason must also be established there, in the substance of the other) through one's influence take seed and grow in the form suited to individuation.[3]

The truth is not learned by reinforcement and habit; it is learned by being in touch with one's own self and by being present to the other, by letting the inner reality contact the outer reality without filtering or censoring perception and awareness.

Another experience essential to man's fulfillment of himself involves the group, that is, three or more persons who come into meaningful interpersonal relations. The group contributes to self-fulfillment in a way that cannot be achieved by the person alone or in person-to-person meetings.

In the presence of widespread breakdown in human communication, distortion, hypocrisy, alienation, and violence and crime, a relatively new movement has emerged, a movement which Carl Rogers has called a potent new cultural development—the intensive group experience. This experience has been called the basic encounter group. The encounter group is a small group, usually about twelve to fifteen members, and relatively unstructured. The group meets in intensive, continuous sessions, running from six hours to a week, often in a retreat setting. It chooses its own goals and directions. The focus is on immediate personal interaction. The leader is important in the initial moments in making orienting comments that provide a beginning structure; later he serves

3. Martin Buber, *The Knowledge of Man*, Maurice Friedman, ed. (New York: Harper & Row, Publishers, 1967), p. 69.

to facilitate the process or becomes a member, leaving the group leaderless.

Hobart Thomas describes the encounter group as follows: ". . . the props are removed and the individual is in a type of 'no exit' situation where he faces himself and others without benefit of the masks behind which he can ordinarily hide. . . . People become freer to express how they really feel toward each other. Generally, negative feelings soon occur. Irritations toward each other are expressed. Roles and game-playing are made more obvious to people, and after a period of time their need to maintain them is lessened. Significant experiences are shared and gradually deep feelings between people emerge."[4]

Rogers believes that the individual will gradually feel safe enough to drop his defenses and begin to relate directly on a feeling basis with other members of the group, that he will understand himself more accurately, will change in personal attitudes and behavior, and will subsequently relate more effectively to others in his everyday life situation. He believes, too, that the group will move from confusion, fractionation, and discontinuity to a climate of trust and coherence. S. I. Hayakawa adds this note:

> I'm fascinated by the degree to which people around here and at Big Sur and in many places around the country are going in for sensitivity training and the heightening of awareness of movement and touch and so on—as if you have to go to seminars to learn this!
>
> I can understand the reason for this preoccupation. Our education is highly verbal. As soon as children get into the

4. Hobart Thomas, "The Encounter Group and Some of Its Implications for Education and Life," Unpublished Paper (Rohnert Park, Calif.: Sonoma State College, 1966), p. 4.

first grade, teachers start verbalizing at them and getting verbal answers back. This training goes on, becoming more and more intensely verbal as you go through high school, college, and graduate school.

Perhaps in a very important sense, as D. H. Lawrence charged, we have lost touch with our passional selves; we have lost the ability to know each other at the nonverbal level, looking at each other's eyes, touching each other's hands and feeling each other's presence and responding to each other—rather than to each other's titles! [5]

Centers are emerging everywhere in the United States and in various parts of the world that not only offer opportunities to participate in encounter groups but unusual, new ways to break down communication barriers, open up long dormant body potentials, create new movements and forms, promote authentic dialogue and multilogue, both verbal and nonverbal, relax frozen muscles, and bring the individual back to his own natural desires and impulses and the group into genuine life. Role-playing, psychodrama, suggested fantasies, directed daydreams, sensory awakening exercises, body awareness techniques, massages, angry encounters—all are used to break through dead patterns in human relations and help people face themselves honestly.

One of the important principles of sensitivity and awareness groups is the recognition of the significance of the body. As long as the body remains an object to the ego, Alexander Lowen explains, as long as it is ignored or transformed into an object by dieting or weight-lifting, though it may fulfill the ego's pride, it will not provide the joy and satisfaction that the "alive" body offers.

5. S. I. Hayakawa, "Interlude Two: How Far Should We Go?" *ETC*, xxv (June, 1968), pp. 213–14.

He also states that: ". . . love and orgasm are *the* irrational experiences we *all* seek. Thus, the person who is afraid of the irrational is afraid of love and orgasm. He is also afraid to let his body go, to let his tears flow and to let his voice break. He is afraid to breathe and afraid to move." [6]

To release bodily tensions the person must learn to breathe more deeply, especially abdominally. Most people breathe only from the neck up; the remainder of the body is dead. The first step is to become aware of the tensions in the body.

Example 1: The person is asked to stand with his feet about thirty inches apart, toes turned inward, knees bent as much as possible, back arched, and hands upon hips. Then he inhales deeply in the abdominal area and slowly, gradually exhales through the diaphragm and nose.

Example 2: In this exercise, which also encourages abdominal breathing, the person places the weight on his feet, which are about fifteen inches apart, with toes turned slightly inward and fingers lightly touching the floor. The knees are always flexed. The degree of flexion varies according to the amount of stress one places on the leg muscle. Persons who assume this position develop a tremor of the legs sooner or later, experienced pleasurably as a sign of life. The position is maintained as long as it produces meaningful sensations in the body.

In *Joy* William C. Schutz offers many possibilities for encounter, body awareness, and sense relaxation. I shall describe some of them:

1. For many people tension is so continuous that they are unaware they are tense. Tension decreases the opportunity for experiencing freely and fully. A simple method to improve

6. Alexander Lowen, *Betrayal of the Body* (New York: The Macmillan Company, 1966), p. 235.

this situation consists in asking everyone in a group to walk slowly in a circle and try to feel as relaxed as possible. Each muscle in the body is gradually tensed, beginning with the face and neck and proceeding through the shoulders, chest, arms, hands, stomach, pelvis, upper legs, lower legs, feet, toes. The tension is increased as much as possible. Finally, the tension is slowly relaxed, beginning from the toes and proceeding upward step-by-step until the head is released.

2. Various childhood problems result in a tightness through the upper respiratory tract and lead to shallow breathing and "tight voice." There is often a stifled desire to shout back at a parental figure but because of a fear of retaliation or withdrawal of love, or from guilt, the scream never comes. The voice remains characteristically quiet and taut.

One method for dealing with this situation is to get the person to scream as loud as he can, over and over again. The effects can sometimes be very dramatic, resulting in crying, raging, and a feeling of great release. If he cannot yell in front of people, the person may be able to yell in the shower or while driving on the highway.

3. It often happens that a tense rib cage constricts breathing and prevents feelings from flowing through the body, often the person lacks vitality and is unable to move freely. The muscles surrounding the rib cage and the lungs may be restored by stretching them to their natural length and by exercising a fullness of breathing. One method instructs two persons to stand back-to-back with their arms stretched high over the head, hands together. The stretcher grabs the hands firmly and dips slightly to ensure that the stretchee's buttocks are next to the small of his back. The stretcher now slowly bends forward until his back is approximately parallel to the ground thus raising the stretchee off the ground. The

stretchee relaxes and breathes heavily through the mouth, sucking in and blowing out. When this rhythm is established the stretcher dips toward the ground during the inhale and rises slightly during the exhale, thus facilitating the deep breathing. When the stretchee has had enough, the stretcher slowly straightens to an upright position.

4. An example of the guided daydream follows:[7]

> I was told to imagine myself in front of a cave. (Guide: The cave has a large door on it and there is something behind the door trying to get out. Go up to the cave, open the door, and see what happens.) The door is heavily bolted and it takes every ounce of strength I have to release it. As I enter, I see two very large eyes bouncing around in the pitch dark of the cave. I am very frightened. (Can you go over to the eyes?) No, I cannot, it is very dark except for a very tiny window throwing a streak of light. Suddenly the room is well-lit. I realize I am standing in the middle of a doll house. The furniture is all very tiny. (Can you go over to the eyes now?) No. (Are they still there?) Yes. They keep bouncing around all about me. I am bewildered and somewhat embarrassed by the small furniture. (What about the eyes, can you approach them now?) No. I am very bothered by them. (Would it be easier if someone were with you?) Yes, I think it would be. (Choose whomever you want.) Suddenly I am aware of someone standing next to me, taking me by the hand, and leading me towards the eyes. It seems so natural, this person is my husband, but I am very upset over the fact that it is. He leads me to the eyes which turn out to be nothing but a large piece of paper on a wall with a drawing of two large cartoon eyes on it. My husband immediately disappears and I pull the

7. William C. Schutz, *Joy* (New York: Grove Press, Inc., 1967), pp. 91–93.

paper from the wall, crumple it, and throw it away. I become very relaxed and somewhat angry at myself as I begin to realize what some of this fantasy is all about. (Would you like to continue in the cave?) No I would much rather leave. It is very bright and sunny outside, and I am very relieved to be there with the smell of fresh air all about me.

One consequence of the fantasy is that it has raised my search for myself to a new level. The "little girl" living with her husband in a doll-house world was not enough. I've become more adult, more willing to try new things, to be with new people, to test myself more. I experience myself as having more guts and as being less awed and less frightened by unfamiliar people and situations. But this process has not been all joy. Having tossed out the little girl, I have lost some of the comfort and support associated with that way of life. Growing up means finding *my* way and this has been and still is a difficult process.

5. The members of a group are asked to sit close together, either on the floor (which is preferable) or in chairs. Then they are asked to close their eyes, stretch out their hands, and feel the space in front of them, over their heads, behind their backs, and below them. They are instructed to be aware of their contact with others as they overlap and begin to touch each other.

6. The suggestion is made for the men in the group to form a closed circle. One person stands in the center and bumps shoulder-to-shoulder in "rooster fight" fashion with each member of the group. It is important that each of the men bump hard or it will not be experienced as a real encounter. As the intensity increases the person in the center often feels a sense of power, release, and satisfaction in bumping against others in a vigorous way.

7. The people identified as "in" stand together in a tight circle and interlock arms. The outsider stands outside the group and tries to break through the circle in whatever way he can. The task of the group members is to keep him out. The outsider must not only break in but also must link arms with the other members of the group.

8. When a conflict exists, e.g., a man and a woman exchanging hostile comments and apparently getting nowhere, they are asked to stop talking but to continue to communicate. The requirement that the participants use only non-verbal communication forces them to employ new tactics. Often new feelings come through and the need for attack and defense is eliminated.

9. When verbalizing gets in the way, the two persons involved are asked to stand at opposite ends of the room. They are instructed to remain silent, look into each other's eyes, and walk very slowly toward each other. When they get close to each other they are to express spontaneously whatever they feel. It is usually more effective when the communications are non-verbal. The couple continue to encounter one another for as long as they wish.

10. Pushing is a useful method in competitive situations where the two people are avoiding direct encounter. The two participants stand facing each other and clasp both hands, palm to palm, intertwining fingers. They push each other, each attempting to make the other give ground, stopping when they both feel satisfied that a real meeting has taken place.

James Bugental and Robert Tannenbaum have listed the following as hopeful outcomes of encounter group experiences:

1. Experiencing personal growth in ways previously assumed to be unattainable.
2. Experiencing a relatedness to all men as personally enriching and enhancing.
3. Experiencing individual uniqueness and personal satisfaction in creativity and self-awareness.
4. Being able to distinguish between realistic limits and neurotic or unrealistic limits to self-growth.
5. Being able to recognize an increasing number of alternatives for the making of good choices.
6. Increasing awareness of and respect for feelings, moods, fantasies, speculation, tenderness, concern, and sharing.

Eva Schindler-Rainman has listed the following as important values of nonverbal communication:

1. Helping people to learn new cues both visible and nonvisible;
2. Learning from nonverbal feedback;
3. Learning to listen to one's own and other people's bodies as a way of receiving internal and external communication and as a way of responding in physical rather than verbal ways;
4. Becoming more sensitive to the nonverbal cues we transmit and receive;
5. Increasing the repertoire of receiving and sending skills;
6. Learning to meet people on a nonverbal level; and
7. Helping people to push out their expressive boundaries and make fuller use of movement, limbs, eyes, facial expressions, body.

I have a number of reservations regarding the authenticity of encounter groups and awareness exercises. My first objection relates to the "realness" of what takes place in groups made up of strangers. How authentic are the interactions? How often are the activities simply games and dramatic expressions which are the appropriate behavior of the "sensitivity" cult? When does the drama end and real life begin? How important are the relationships formed in encounter groups? Does the person whom I've just met in quick intimate exchanges, once more become a stranger when the three minutes of encounter are over? Is the experience of pushing or embracing another person authentic when I am told to do so by a trainer? What is the difference between the natural awakening to joy in the presence of others and what occurs when I am told that for the next five minutes I must be nonverbally joyous with three or four others? Having experienced encounter, awareness and sensitivity techniques many times in many different groups, these methods often appear to me to be manipulating and staging maneuvers. Frequently all the persons in a group are expected to participate in the same activity. It is one thing for a leader *to suggest* a method of encountering, it is another to insist that all persons engage in it.

Pursuing further the question of authenticity, I have other doubts about the genuineness of some of the interactions that occur in encounter groups. The sudden anger that is sometimes expressed on the basis of very brief contact with others, within minutes after a group is underway, has seemed to me theatrical. I've been struck by how quickly intense feelings are generated. For instance, in one of my groups, after a young schoolteacher had spoken briefly, a psychiatrist stood up, pointed angrily, and with wild gestures told her that her voice sickened him, that every time she opened her mouth it was like a bucket of honey splashed against his face. In another group, a newspaper writer, after we had gathered for only ten minutes, indicated that he had never felt so warm, close, or intimate with any group before. In a third group, within the first hour, a woman burst into profuse crying, and while three others in the group cuddled and held her, she said she had not wept for years and that the love and acceptance of the group made it possible for her to shed the tears that she had suppressed at her mother's funeral. In each of these situations, the group was made up of people who were strangers to one another. As these encounters continued I came to see that the highly dramatic openings were often delivered by veteran encounter participants—men and women who had been in many groups before. I had the impression that they were putting us on with techniques of confrontation, with ways of expressing and evoking intense emotions, and with gestures that were highly colorful; in other words, infusing in our group a whole range of intense emotional expressions that would have an impact and move others to respond passionately. The nature of the approach makes it difficult to know what is actually a bitter attack or painful anguish and what is simply often-performed theater.

Encounter groups deteriorate into dramatic emotional binges when relatively insignificant matters dominate the attention and life of the group. I am convinced that the color of a person's eyes, the way he combs his hair, his manner of speech, the movement of his body, and similar characteristics are not worth the intense, often agonizing feelings they engender when they become the focus of the group process. Analytical feedback, explanations, and so-called truths about another person's self often are no more than intellectual acrobatics. Rarely do such verbalizations lead to honest interchange. If unauthentic or phony expressions are to be challenged and uprooted, they should be essential, central features of the individual, not the superficial factors that sensitivity groups too often dwell on and labor over.

Further, there is an injustice in confronting or attacking a person I do not know or care to know. I have seen many people hurt by encounters that grew out of theories and techniques rather than from genuine concerns. I increasingly believe that one must earn the right to question the existence of another person and that this right is earned when there is a basic feeling of regard and a desire to establish a relationship. Perhaps the challenge or attack is the only way, but who is to say what is honest and true for another human being. My honesty about someone else is still an external, imposed perception; and though the expression of honesty may be needed to open a path to a full life with the other person, it is more appropriately regarded as a potential bridge to new life, rather than a question of honesty.

I see the value of sensitivity and encounter approaches when they are used spontaneously in a particular group, when the group is ready to experiment with them, when each person is free to respond in his own way, whether he participates or not. If people are restless and want to move, suggestions for exercise and body expression may be helpful; if people are wordy and not communicating honestly, a direct confrontation may be all that is necessary; if people are moved to intimate expression but are fearful or inhibited, they might welcome an opportunity for physical contact and may need the direction of a sensitive guide; if people are initiating dishonest words, an immediate expression of dissatisfaction and protest can be made; if encounters are not completed, any person may interrupt and call this out.

In countless ways, sensitivity techniques can have an important place in fostering authentic communication, heightened self-awareness, and intimacy and trust in relations with others. But as I see it, these methods are only catalysts of temporary value in breaking down barriers; life does not stop there; the essence of human affairs requires much, much more in the way of sharing and struggle in varied experiences.

An additional objection relates to the physical violence that is being employed in some groups, presumably as the only way of dealing with certain problems between group members or between the leader and a member. I am opposed to physical violence on any grounds. I believe that it is a detrimental and destructive approach and, taken to its ultimate level, can only result in irreparable damage. The verbal attacks, however horrible they may be in creating misery and suffering, are always potentially correctable, but loss of an eye is a permanent injury. Once the forces of physical violence are unleashed, the risks and dangers of severe, uncontrollable attack are always present. No person has the right to take the life of another in his own hands. Peace and love among human beings does not result from war. Physical tensions and rages between persons can be released in many ways, but direct physical attack is never justifiable. A group that uses physical violence often idolizes excitement and drama in human affairs, seeks quick solutions to pain and discomfort, and is so imbued with techniques that it has lost touch with underlying principles and values.

One of the major gains of sensitivity and encounter group experience is the acquisition of interpersonal competence. Four criteria of interpersonal competence are identified by Chris Argyris:

1. The individual perceives the interpersonal situation

accurately and is able to identify relevant variables and interrelationships.

2. The individual is able to solve problems so that they remain solved.

3. The solution is achieved in such a way that the persons can continue to work together at least as effectively as when they began to solve the problem.

4. The changes in feeling and thinking can be transferred to new situations. Observable changes can be found in solving interpersonal problems, outside the original learning situation.

These gains in interpersonal competence are not only dependent upon openness, trust, acceptance, and level of awareness but are determined to a great degree by the nature and quality of feedback. A major problem with feedback is that it is very rarely unitary in the group so that the strongest, angriest, or most repetitive voices tend to have undue influence on self-awareness. Also, feedback may be so varied as to become confusing; in other words, the individual may not be able to fit what he hears into his own perceptions and experiences. Ultimately, the person must decide for himself what represents valid impressions and reactions and what is influenced by group contagion or by the forceful reactions of one or a few others.

Sometimes the sensitivity and encounter techniques can be shortcuts to human values; but more often these values can be achieved only by the struggle, frustration, persistent effort, and exertion that comes from within oneself and from continuing interactions with others. The direct path is not always the deepest or most significant one to follow. Detours have their messages and meanings. When truth and reality are at stake, it is often more frustrating and riskier to move in spiral fashion, but the eventual gains are more rewarding and enduring.

Perhaps I can convey my concerns with reference to encounter groups by presenting, in modified form, a letter written after hours of loneliness and solitude. The experience still seems alive and fresh within me and expresses what I currently see as values and limits of encounter groups.

> I see values in people meeting in groups for intense emotional confrontation, but I have reservations about certain aspects of the encounter group. First of all, I think it is a false assumption that people inevitably experience hatred and hostility when they are intimately involved with others. I do not believe that countering hatred and hostility with hatred and hostility always leads to an honest, healthy relationship even when the intentions are good. I also think that individuals engaged in combat must be fairly well matched or there is danger that the weaker opponent will be vanquished and destroyed. In any event, when the opponents are unbalanced, when the strong easily vanquish the weak, there is no real challenge, no real contest. Further, I do not believe that survival of the fittest is a healthy basis for human society (not even in an arena) though it may make sense in the jungle.
>
> I believe it is possible for a person to meet hostility and hatred with pain and suffering, to absorb the blows and the sting of words, and through suffering to maintain his identity, his sensitivity, and to emerge from such a confrontation stronger. In other words, encounter groups know how to use hostility as a force in authenticating life but have not recognized the restorative powers of pain and suffering. Whereas hostile exchange is seen as a step toward genuineness in communication, and thus as a good, pain is seen as corrosive and evil. Reception of hostility with pain

is regarded as a deterrent to the deeper interpersonal process. This need not be so; in fact, it is not so in many interhuman conflicts. . . .

If an individual, who is hanging on to a fragile identity, begins to believe what others say of him and substitutes their definitions of who he is for his own self-image, then is the "love" which may follow nothing more than approval and reward for submission and surrender? And in such an "encounter," who is being loved when there is no one to love? Isn't this what often happens to a child growing up in his family when parents begin to define who the child is and reinforce their definitions with rewards and approval? "If real success is to attend the effort to bring a man to a definite position," says Kierkegaard, "one must first of all take pains to find HIM where he is and begin there. . . . the helper must first humble himself under him he would help, and therewith must understand that to help does not mean to be sovereign but to be servant, that to help does not mean to be ambitious but to be patient, that to help means to endure for the time being the imputation that one is in the wrong and does not understand what the other understands. . . . Instruction begins when you, the teacher, learn from the learner, put yourself in his place so that you may understand what he understands and in the way he understands it."

I know from my own experience in the Esalen encounter group that I met Kris in a way that would not have occurred otherwise. He was one person in the group of whom I was only slightly aware until the basic encounter meetings. But in all the critical and rejecting comments he made to me that night and the next morning I did not feel hostile or rejecting in turn. Inside, I was sweating, biting my mouth, cutting and hurting in some drastic ways. I received what he said but in those moments I felt entirely alone. We were in two different worlds, facing each other but on very dif-

ferent paths, without dialogue—subterranean or otherwise.
I met Kris's hostility with pain and anguish. I absorbed it
and inside me for a while it was like a poison. But, at least,
now he was tangibly present and very real. Until those moments of confrontation, he was another person, vague and
undifferentiated. But once we met head on and he condemned me as a detached intellectual, when he repeatedly
blasted away at me, the pain I experienced enabled me to
stay with my own perceptions and not be carried away by
the sweeping attacks that did not fit my own inner life. In
the end, when all others were gone and I walked without
direction, not knowing where I was or where I was going,
but alone and lonely, Kris and I met on the same path. We
were traveling in different directions and I looked up and
suddenly he was there. We converged in that moment, our
eyes met, and I felt deeply his compassion. He embraced
me and between us there was no more horror; he wept painfully for long, long minutes. And though I was overwhelmed
at the suddenness, extremeness, and totality of the moment,
I felt something deep inside—not just compassion, for I experienced that with him many times that Saturday night,
but a human intimacy and depth, and tears of sadness and
of joy, which washed away the darkness and the gloom.
Then quickly he was moving down a hill and something
warm and shiny and glistening beamed between us; I knew
unexpectedly that we had shared a moment of absolute
communion. Then, only then, was he wholly real to me—
when we stood there on the same path and we were alone,
person-to-person; it was unlike any moment with him in
the group.

I believe in the value of transcendence. Many times in
my life I have overcome obstacles to my own growth; I have
discovered resources when none appeared available, and I
have met many, many people who by all the facts which
surrounded them should have been miserable, destructive,

limited people but who, on the contrary, were vital, alive,
wondrous, joyful people. Many times, too, I have felt emptiness, boredom, triviality, repetitiveness, sterility, and mean-
inglessness—but when I transcended the mood or feeling
or situation, when I became involved, spontaneous and free,
when I focused on other aspects of my experience, suddenly
I was seeing with different eyes and hearing with different
ears. Who knows, who can tell what may happen next—
waiting has its value in this and intention and belief, and
then (it has no rational basis) boredom dissipates into interest, sadness into joy, emptiness into excitement. I think
of Frankl's concentration camp victims. With all the brutality, cruelty, hatred, torture, disease, hunger, and cold, they
still maintained their altruism, their love, sharing their last
piece of bread, enduring terrible agony, handing over their
last shred of clothing, freezing, but still serving the maimed,
the dying, and the deteriorating people around them.

If the meditative, reflective processes are not recognized
and respected, then the battles and conflicts which emerge
rest not on the real issues between man and man but on
false theories, false threats, and false assumptions. Kierkegaard wrote in one of his journals: "There is a view of life
which conceives that where the crowd is, there also is the
truth, and that in truth itself there is need of having the
crowd on its side . . . a crowd in its very concept is the
untruth, by reason of the fact that it renders the individual
completely impenitent and irresponsible, or at least weakens
his sense of responsibility by reducing it to a fraction. . . .
No, when it is a question of a single individual man, then is
the time to give expression to the truth by showing one's
respect for what it is to be a man."

Under certain conditions, within a certain climate, where
the basic intentions are positive and underlying value is
present, love can emerge in a group. Then persons can know
turbulence with one another, in challenge and contest, in

struggle and encounter. At the same time, within the group there must develop a basic sympathy and regard. I have learned from this that, for some people, *only* through combat can hostility be dissipated; *only* through countering hatred with hatred, openly, directly, clearly, and simply, can growth be achieved. I saw emerging guilt and anxiety move people to suffer, to atone, and to experience genuine feeling for one another. Through a battle in open, honest challenge, men can experience an eventual toughness and an essential caring. But it is not the only way and it is not always the preferred way.

Why must some people counter hatred with hatred in order to become genuinely involved? What happens in that single, solitary moment to bring about the radical shift from hostile criticism to compassion and love? It looks like such a turnabout of extremes—but is it? What are the conditions which facilitate the battle but keep the lines of attack, the opposing forces, enough in balance so that no one is overwhelmed, defeated, or totally crushed, so that at no point is there a point of no return, so that no one fails to get back up and face the ordeal? How can encounter groups recognize the value of privacy and not interfere with the individual's solitary moments, not impede self-awareness, which depends solely on the person's own struggles with himself? What kind of climate facilitates the exchange and keeps people together and the contest a verbal battle? And what underlying theme or value keeps alive the growth dimensions in these meetings when destructive words and gestures, resentment, sarcasm, bitterness, meanness, and other forms of evil are central signs?

I know the encounter group has value in some situations with some people, but I'm searching for the kind of awareness that for me will make it a living reality, where all three structures are recognized and valued: solitude and loneliness, person-to-person dialogue, and intense group experience.

I think the encounter group represents a new perspective that may clear the way for many of us struggling for authentic life with others. But I also believe that the essential uniqueness, the elemental otherness of each person must be recognized and that moments of self-dialogue and private self-reflection must be respected in every human setting. The precept, "If you can't make it with people you can't make it," has a corollary: "If you can only make it with people, and not alone, you can't make it."

references

ARGYRIS, CHRIS. "Conditions for Competence Acquisition and Therapy." *Journal of Applied Behavioral Science,* IV (1968), 147–77.

BATCHELDER, RICHARD L., and HARDY, JAMES M. *Using Sensitivity Training and the Laboratory Method.* New York: Association Press, 1968.

BRADFORD, LELAND P., GIBB, JACK R., and BENNE, KENNETH D., eds. *T-Group Theory and Laboratory Method.* New York: John Wiley & Sons, Inc., 1964.

BUBER, MARTIN. *Between Man and Man.* Tr. Ronald Gregor Smith. Boston: Beacon Press, 1955.

——. *The Knowledge of Man.* Maurice Friedman, ed. New York: Harper & Row, Publishers, 1967.

BUGENTAL, JAMES F. T., and TANNENBAUM, ROBERT. "Sensitivity Training and Being Motivation." *Journal of Humanistic Psychology,* III (Spring, 1968), 76–85.

BYRD, RICHARD E. "Training in a Non-Group." *Journal of Humanistic Psychology,* VII (Spring, 1967), 18–27.

COOPER, C. L., and MANGHAM, I. L., eds. *T-Groups: A Survey of Research*. London: Wiley & Sons Ltd., 1971.

FRANKL, VIKTOR E. *Man's Search for Meaning*. New York: Washington Square Press, 1963.

GREENE, MAXINE. *Existential Encounters for Teachers*. New York: Random House, Inc., 1967.

GUNTHER, BERNARD. *Sense Relaxation*. New York: The Macmillan Company, 1968.

HAYAKAWA, S. I. "Interlogue Two: How Far Should We Go?" *ETC*, XXV (June, 1968), 209–21.

KEEN, SAM. *To A Dancing God*. New York: Harper & Row, Publishers, 1970.

KIERKEGAARD, SOREN. *The Journals*. New York: Harper & Row, Publishers, Harper Torchbooks, 1959.

———. *The Point of View for My Work as an Author*. New York: Harper & Row, Publishers, Harper Torchbooks, 1959.

LEONARD, GEORGE B. *Education and Ecstasy*. New York: Delacorte Press, 1968.

LOWEN, ALEXANDER. *Betrayal of the Body*. New York: The Macmillan Company, 1966.

LYON, HAROLD C. *Learning to Feel—Feeling to Learn*. Columbus, Ohio: Charles E. Merrill Publishing Co., 1971.

MARCEL, GABRIEL. *The Mystery of Being*, Vol. I. Chicago: Henry Regnery Co., 1951.

MASLOW, ABRAHAM H. *Eupsychian Management*. Homewood, Ill.: Dorsey, 1965.

MORENO, J. L. "The Viennese Origins of the Encounter Movement." *Group Psychotherapy*, XXII (1969), 7–16.

MOUSTAKAS, CLARK. *Individuality and Encounter*. Cambridge, Mass.: Howard Doyle Publishing Co., 1968.

NIETZSCHE, FRIEDRICH. *Thus Spake Zarathustra.* In *The Portable Nietzsche,* Walter Kaufman, ed. New York: The Viking Press, 1954.

ORTEGA Y GASSET, JOSE. *Man and People.* New York: W. W. Norton & Co., Inc., Norton Library, 1957.

PERLS, FRITZ. *Gestalt Therapy Verbatim.* Lafayette, Calif.: Real People Press, 1969.

ROGERS, CARL R. "The Process of the Basic Encounter Group." Unpublished paper. La Jolla, Calif.: Western Behavioral Sciences Institute, 1966.

———. *Carl Rogers on Encounter Groups.* New York: Harper & Row, Publishers, 1970.

SCHINDLER-RAINMAN, EVA. "The Importance of Non-Verbal Communication in Laboratory Training." *Adult Leadership,* XVI (April, 1968), 357–358.

SCHUTZ, WILLIAM C. *Joy: Expanding Human Awareness.* New York: Grove Press, Inc., 1967.

THOMAS, HOBART F. "The Encounter Group and Some of Its Implications for Education and Life." Unpublished paper. Rohnert Park, Calif.: Sonoma State College, 1966.

ZWEBEN, JOAN E., and HAMMANN, KALEN. "Prescribed Games." *Psychotherapy,* VII (Spring, 1970), 22–27.

6 | *the individual versus the group*

Sometimes it is difficult to know who I am, yet other voices are always available and ready to define and explain me. Being myself was once a simple matter but, with increasing involvement in groups, I am no longer as spontaneously certain. Part of this doubt comes from the feedback and pronouncements I receive: "you are exclusive," "you are overly refined," "you are too blunt," "you care too much," "you don't even know I exist," "you're too powerful," "you need to develop more strength," "you're much too sensitive," "you are not sensitive enough," "I like your moustache," "I don't like your moustache," "you make moralistic judgments," "you're never willing to make judgments," "your religious mysticism frightens me," "your atheism is the reason I distrust you," "you do not provide enough leadership," "you're too direct."

Am I really so radically different for different persons? Am I that inconsistent and changeable? How is it that I am perceived in these opposite ways?

As long as others accept my own self-perceptions as valid,

no conflict occurs; but when my self-perceptions differ from what others see, if I persist in maintaining myself, it is inevitable that I will be questioned, challenged, and sometimes rejected. Perhaps a balance can be achieved that does not depend solely on my own perceptions of myself but includes the feedback of others. When I am not in touch with myself, the perceptions of others may help to point the way. However, I see this direction in self-awareness as an occasional movement from the outside in. It is my conviction that the essential patterns of personal growth remain from the inside out. In the ultimate moment I must stand by my own senses and continue to believe what I see, feel, hear, and touch. My own experience is real no matter what others say and no matter how many there are to say it. The final judgment is my own, although at any point along the way I hope I am open enough to learn from the experiences of others.

This emphasis on maintaining one's identity is powerfully expressed in Eldridge Cleaver's letter to Beverly Axelrod:

> Let me say this. I was 22 when I came to prison and of course I have changed tremendously over the years. But I had always had a strong sense of myself and in the last few years I felt I was losing my identity. There was a deadness in my body that eluded me, as though I could not exactly locate its site. I would be aware of this numbness, this feeling of atrophy, and it haunted the back of my mind. Because of this numb spot, I felt peculiarly off balance, the awareness of something missing, of a blank spot, a certain intimation of emptiness. Now I know what it was. And since encountering you, I feel life strength flowing back into that spot. My step, the tread of my stride, which was becoming tentative and uncertain, has begun to recover and take on a new definiteness, a confidence, a boldness which makes me want to kick over a few tables. I may even swagger a little,

and, as I read in a book somewhere, "push myself forward like a train." [1]

Sometimes I wonder how others can be so sure and unqualified in their perceptions when I am often groping to determine who I am, especially when I am encountering new people. How is it that I need time to consider while others often quickly decide and talk as if they knew me better than I know myself? When there is an issue, when self and others are at odds, the situation is rarely resolved through a quick insight. When change is instantaneous, it is more likely that new thoughts or feelings are being taken on, rather than taken in as essential ingredients of oneself. Group pressures to perceive more validly and more effectively are not helpful when they direct the way. The individual is helped only when he is encouraged to enter his own solitary world for awhile and stay with himself until he reaches his own clarity and sense of direction. It may be possible for this private search to take place in the group, or it may be necessary for the person to withdraw to a quiet place.

Self-reflection is often rejected in a group, even when it is obvious that the person needs to stay with himself. The individual is pushed to disclose what is happening within before he knows himself. When the person experiences the pressure and becomes agitated or frightened, he no longer hears himself or feels his thoughts and feelings; he no longer knows what is real. To make his peace with others he may resort to dramatic tactics or he may capitulate and do what is expected. Within the group, the individual needs time to catch his breath; he needs time to consider, explore, and pursue inner thoughts and feelings. When group members

1. Eldridge Cleaver, *Soul on Ice* (New York: Dell Publishing Co., 1968), pp. 143–44.

badger, demand, and quickly formulate statements, when a powerful emotional force is directed against the solitary person, the individual becomes more involved in the emotional charges than in his own search for truth. Individual awareness may move more slowly than group awareness, but ultimately it is the only reality that makes sense. The person should be free to decide whether he wishes to pursue his identity in the group or alone, and his decision should be respected.

At times, the individual must learn to listen to others if he is to have clearer, more comprehensive awareness of himself; but it is also essential that group members learn to listen to the individual in order to know when to provoke, protest, and challenge and when to pause and give the person an opportunity to sink into himself. Perhaps, to enable the group to move on, a temporary solution must satisfy; thus direct encounter and sensitivity techniques are a quick and effective means. However, the group should know that the real issues in self-growth have been bypassed and that if enduring changes are to occur the person or persons involved must struggle further. An overly verbal person does not eliminate his excessive use of words through group pressures and denial. He may get the kind of jolt that will silence him temporarily, but real change is tested in day-to-day living not in enforced silence, not through tactics that suppress the individual.

It is much more difficult for a group to convince itself that it has made a mistake in its perceptions of a person than it is for an individual, with prodding from a group, to realize that he needs to correct his understanding of himself. Yet if growth is to take place, the group must also be alert to its own distortions, its unjust pronouncements, and its misunderstandings. When an individual is at odds with a group, it is just as necessary for the group to reflect on its version of truth and reality as it is for the individual.

Individual values are reconcilable with group values, but to achieve a cooperative interplay each must be recognized, respected, and given opportunity for expression. Leaders of groups must be concerned with enabling individuals to discover themselves and be more fully aware of who they are as they develop a sense of cohesiveness and unity in a group. Otherwise, the apparent unity may be a sophisticated type of conformity, with members more eager for status, recognition, and approval than for honest inquiry and exchange. A recent study concluded that members who perceived themselves to be influential and proficient in carrying out group functions were well-liked by group members, and were more satisfied with the group. Such persons obviously are more committed to being liked and to carrying out group values than they are with truth and reality in the lives of individual persons.

A person's journey into himself is the most direct way to a real life with others. Something in his life is missing, something is lost. His search is a beginning, a chance to recover and to express what appears irretrievable. In such a moment everything depends on the affirmation and silence of the group. In such a moment, as a friend put it, "loving allowances" are required; an attack more than anything else may bury deeper that something lost within.

Each person, however fixed or set, is on his way to becoming a new being with others. What he expresses at any single moment is valid and real in its own right; it leads to the next moment in his growth. Without this expression, which at the moment does not seem significant to others, the person cannot become what he is capable of becoming. When rejected, the immediate expression remains fixed, held on to, protected. By letting the individual be, by letting him enter in his own time, he may become a real member of the group. But if he is threatened or attacked, if he is denied and ignored, he may withdraw permanently or, at best, simulate accommodation to the group.

Thus, the real challenge for the group is to commit itself to the individual, to remain with an individual even when his search does not seem immediately relevant to the group as a whole. On the other hand, at times, the individual must transcend his own private world and trust in a process that has no immediate value. Specifically, this kind of transcendence means a commitment to every person in the group. It is a transcendence of the concrete and the particular, and an entering into the lives of others with determination and faith.

Perhaps the most important aspect of the struggle between the individual and the group is the willingness to wait, to be patient, and to "waste" time with each individual while somehow keeping the exchange alive. What comes in the first burst of expression and response may not be immediately meaningful, but it is a first step and needs to be approached more with the attitude "There's all the time in the world" than with "Every moment is precious; let's get at the issues quickly." Part of this process of meaningful inquiry, self-searching, and development of significant interpersonal relations involves wasting time—that is, the willingness to let the person emerge, stand out in his own way, with his own voice and style of expression; the willingness to let the pace fit the individual, the willingness of the group to let itself unfold in a way that is consistent with the particular persons who constitute it. Wasting time in this sense is not a negative use of energy and talent but rather it is a way of life in which the individual gradually reveals himself and begins to want to know other persons. This process of waiting, of being patient, and of being willing to waste time produces results that are more real and enduring. The process is one of letting what is be, of permitting the person to emerge and unfold in his own pattern and style. Others help this process by encouraging the individual to stay on his own path, not by attacking or condemning his uniqueness, but by guiding the false or external impulses back to an authentic path. Once on that path, the person should be free to proceed at his own rate and with his own idiosyncracies. In time, he may reach a place of tranquility; the wild, inner confusions and furies may be released and tamed.

To "tame" another human being need not be an authoritarian process. In the sense of *The Little Prince* it does not mean to make docile or tractable, or to crush, subdue, and make deficient in spirit, or to tone down and soften, as happens so often when an individual stands out strongly and threatens the shaky unity of the group. To tame the individual means to establish ties with him. This means a willingness to enter his life and to respect his unique requirements. To tame means to be willing to waste time, not to be in a hurry, but to come to value just being with the person. "Men have forgotten this truth," said the fox. "But you must not forgot it. You become responsible, forever, for what you have tamed."

I believe that the most significant and valid way to group life lies in individual experience. The essential aspects of an authentic community of persons are: a respect for both individual and group values, a willingness to give and take, a determination to transcend, and patience to stay with the moment until a natural stopping, if not closure, is achieved. In my experience, the potential for synergy is always present. Synergy is experienced through the increasing realization of both individuality and community in a group; eventually individual fulfillment and group fulfillment become synonymous. Whether it develops or not depends on whether the inherent conflicts between individual and group can be resolved. However, the complexity of conditions and the diversity of individuals generally prevent the ideal community from being fully realized. But it is a deeply satisfying experience when a sense of unity and integration occurs at points along the way.

I have been in groups that were so "group-oriented" that it was extremely difficult for the individual to say "yes" or "no," to give his own verdict on the experience, to let issues remain unfinished, or to reflect privately and remain silent. I have also been in groups where there was no commitment to a group process, where once the individual's needs were met he became essentially uncommitted and unresponsive to what was happening to others.

Two of the most disappointing experiences I have had in groups have been oriented toward the extremes of the individual or the group. In one, the group as a whole was so geared to drama that every moment had to contain emotional catharsis and fireworks or the members became restless or sleepy. To keep the group awake and intensely involved, several members used hostile encounters—attacking, belittling, shaming, minimizing; they also used body tactics—touching, exploring, embracing. This group stayed together constantly in a kind of combined shock therapy-love-in. In the end most members valued their experiences—the angry screaming, the painful weeping, the affectionate embraces, the holding hands, and the pounding, pushing, yelling, role-playing, and guided daydreams. But along the way a number of individuals were lost; some were deeply hurt and struggled with the crushing attacks; or they were confused by the intense embraces. Some were more hardened and detached, some became withdrawn and isolated. The majority had been involved in the main action all the way, immersed in the exciting, tangible dramas. Although I could see the significance of what was happening for the majority (and in some ways I valued and participated in these experiences), I left the group somewhat discouraged because sometimes the peak moments were achieved at the expense of individuals, some of whom finished the week-end more diminished than when it started.

At the other extreme was a group with many self-centered persons, each of whom wanted to be the focus of attention, each of whom wanted opportunities to explore his own personal problems and to communicate his negative feelings. They were involved in the life of the group only as long as it centered on them; but the minute the subject changed they talked to neighbors, yawned or slept, and often disrupted the process by going out for coffee and snacks or leaving the room altogether. One by one, each person in this group had his time in the spotlight, but departed as soon as another person struggled to express his inner concerns. I had been with one individual after another hour after hour, and when the early morning came, I got a tremendous jolt. I was so immersed in the last person's effort to recover the joy and laughter of his childhood that I was completely unaware of what had happened in the room. When I looked up, to my surprise I was entirely alone. It was the most crushing experience I have had in a group. I felt no elation that each person might have found something of value for himself. The failure of any real connection to emerge between individuals on some important level was a severe blow. I too moved out quickly and drove away, discouraged, defeated, and depressed.

I do not hope to achieve the individual-communal ideal in every group experience or an I-Thou connection with each person; but without development of unity, mutuality, valuing of self and other on some level, the struggle to know oneself and to know other persons does not move forward. When unity of self and other is experienced and communication reaches a heightened, personal meaning, life is being lived at a peak level. At times it seems unbelievable, almost beyond reach, but when it happens it is something of awesome beauty.

references

CLEAVER, ELDRIDGE. *Soul on Ice*. New York: Dell Publishing Co., 1968.

MASLOW, A. H. *Toward a Psychology of Being*. Princeton, N.J.: D. Van Nostrand Co., Inc., 1962.

MOUSTAKAS, CLARK. *Individuality and Encounter*. Cambridge, Mass.: Howard Doyle Publishing Co., 1968.

SAINT EXUPERY, ANTOINE DE. *The Little Prince*. New York: Harcourt, Brace & World, Inc., 1953.

7 | *honesty
versus
truth*

I became seriously involved in the issue of honesty vs. truth after considerable conflict and struggle in encounter groups, where I had been criticized for not being aggressive and combative in my communications with others. I was told that to be an effective leader—more than this—to live a full life, I needed to become more forceful; I needed to learn how to facilitate the expression of anger in myself and others. Since conflicts were inevitable in the intensive group process, it was up to me to ferret them out, evoke them, and through my own angry exchanges with others serve as a model in pointing the way. Since these instructions did not fit my own perception of what was required, I had to choose between remaining myself or following an alien path. A period of self-reflection resulted in a decision to test out the instructions, experiment with myself, and find out who I could become in angry confrontation. What would it be like to enter a group with the serious intention of becoming angry and challenging and pursuing others in my anger?

Expression of anger was not a new experience for me, but

I almost never engaged in angry outbursts with strangers or in new relationships. On the rare occasions in which I really felt heated anger, it was directed toward persons with whom I had ties—my wife, my sons, and friends of long standing. My anger was not communicated in a violent or hostile form; there was no desire or intention to crush, defeat, or destroy. I grew up in a family of basically gentle people where differences were resolved through a silent search within and struggle in solitude, through transcendence, and by plunging into new experiences—where the tension and conflict dissipated with time, and living with the pain somehow healed the wound. Every family relationship—my mother, my father, my brothers and sisters—was maintained and enriched; there was not a single instance of a permanent break; on the contrary, there was depth, significance, and love in each relationship. With each conflict, I ultimately came to trust and to be trusted. I came to see myself as a tender but strong person, who could be tough when it was necessary; who could persist with determination in the face of obstacles, threats, and challenges. I saw myself as a person who often chose the hard path because it required me to stretch myself, tax my energies, and fully use my resources in meeting the requirements of a new path or the essentials of a new life. In these ways I felt my strength as a person, a strength that grew essentially from encounters and challenges with myself, and from my willingness and determination to stay with controversy and conflict, no matter what, and to maintain my faith and belief in the restorative possibilities of life. I had no evidence that the conflict between myself and others would end peacefully, or result in deeper ties.

My introduction to encounter groups threatened these

patterns and perceptions of myself. The feedback I got from some strong voices cast doubt in me. I began to question the pattern formed early in my family life; I began to doubt what I had always felt to be an authentic expression of me. After a number of confrontations in which others tried to arouse anger in me, I decided that the next time I felt irritation or annoyance I would open up with whatever abusive language was in me. The first time the vehemence in my voice frightened and shocked me. The words, sounds, and visual expressions were me and yet not me. I actually felt anger at the moment; it was real; yet it was superficial rather than deep—something fleeting, rather than enduring or pressing; it was something I could hang on to or let go. Since the experiment required that I focus on and accentuate my anger, I stayed with it. The persons who received my anger were really hurt, and for many hours in these groups I worked to lessen the pain that I had helped to create. The power of my caustic remarks hit the target hard; and sometimes, even when the encounter group came to a close, I felt that my victim had become a diminished human being, that his spirit had noticeably dwindled. Even so, I sharpened my skills in angry communication; and in time I developed an ability to attack and criticize, to express feelings of disappointment, irritation, and dissatisfaction at whatever I regarded as phony, dishonest, manipulating, shallow, weak. I became more competent in shattering habits and patterns of communication, in pounding away at the games and tactics people used, in forcefully cutting into stalemates and barriers to an authentic life. But the consequence for me was a feeling of exhaustion and deadness in my own spirit. I felt worn out from putting the pieces back together and attempting to heal the wounds I had helped to make. I began to wonder whether I really wanted to live in this way, whether I should continue to meet with groups at all.

Throughout this period I often experienced a sickness in myself. Because I was the leader, my angry expressions had a particularly strong impact. I was supposed to be in touch with reality and truth. I was seen as a person of authority, in spite of the fact that my anger was expressed as a personal, individual response. For about six months, momentary honesty in angry encounters ruled my life with people. Though the anger was expressed in only a few minutes, it took several hours to deal with its consequences. The meetings were often exciting, dramatic, and alive but there were consequences. I sometimes experienced stomach pains, body tensions, headaches, loss of appetite, and disturbed sleep. Something was wrong, radically wrong in my communications and relationships. The sickness reached a peak one day in an encounter with a colleague who later reported that she did not sleep for two nights, and that my angry communication had disturbed her relationship with her husband and daughter. I could clearly see the upheaval and havoc I was causing in other people's lives. Were these angry encounters necessary for authentic living and growing? I found it hard to justify the bad vibrations and the eventual pain and suffering on the basis of the honesty of my anger. I began to question what I really wanted in my communications with others and felt myself to be increasingly alienated, that I was going against my own senses. What was the real value of honesty? What was happening to me in these new emotional outbursts?

I realized when I began to consider the meaning of anger in my life that I have always been reluctant to hurt others because I know what it feels like to be criticized and attacked, I know what it means to be hurt. But this had nothing to do with any squeamishness in expressing anger or with any inner weakness that made it difficult to meet others on strong terms. I began to see that there were deeper questions: Who am I? What do I seek in my life with others? What are my values, ideals, desires? I began to realize something rather obvious. I always have a choice—and my choices are based on my preferences and values. In choosing to express momentary honest anger, I had listened to other voices express what mattered to them. I had listened to others telling of their restraints and blocks in relationships. I had been influenced by what others found to be effective for themselves, I had stopped listening to myself and stopped trusting my own experience. I had abandoned a vital pattern of my being, a pattern rooted in my past but, until the encounter group involvement, very satisfying in the present and valuable for the future. In short, I had abandoned my old self and tried to develop a new self based on avoiding what others saw as a weakness or gap. When my life in the group became continually exhausting and began to follow a pattern of angry outbursts—pain—suffering—comforting—healing, I began to yearn for my earlier, simpler, and more satisfying life with others, a way of life that did not require such a heavy investment of energy in zeroing in on conflict and then concentrating on it in order to resolve it. In retreat with myself, I questioned the "anger formula" that I had been told was essential to a significant group process. I came to see that my body tensions and headaches were a protest against the denial of my own self. Thus, while I was being "honest" in the moment when I angrily confronted other people, my honesty was often a lie in the sense that it denied something essential in me, something rooted in the values and ways of my life. The angry outbursts denied an ideal in the present and a value to live by in the future.

I no longer believe that an angry encounter always serves the persons involved. It can block, restrain, and close a person so that a process of struggle and searching is terminated, so that openness and trust turn to fear and suspicion, so that the persons involved become cautious, begin to play games with one another, and even wear masks of supersensitivity and concern. One of R. D. Laing's "knots" expresses the clever bargain that people make, "They are playing a game. They are playing at not playing a game. If I show them I see they are, I shall break the rules and they will punish me. I must play their game, of not seeing I see the game." [1]

I discovered in an exciting and personal way that I am much more dedicated to truth than to honesty; and when I choose honesty over truth—when these two values are in conflict—I am going against myself and against what I value more in life. In a sense I am not being myself at my deepest, most profound level of being. Thus my honesty is a lie. Gentle ways are more basically rooted in me. Sometimes, the preferred choice is difficult to make. The upheaval and the anger seem to be necessary steps back to a gentle orientation, but this is the exception, not a basic pattern. I discovered in my search that when anger endures, or when any feeling continues to exist over time, it is dependable—it is not only honest but true. Whenever I am not being myself (for example, when I am acting on other people's standards, expectations, or pressures or when I am extremely tired or ill) and I immediately express what I am feeling, though the feelings are actually present and honest, they are not true. I actually feel anger, sadness, or joy but these feelings are the outcome

1. R. D. Laing, *Knots* (New York: Pantheon Books, 1970).

of temporary pressures and influences; they are not basic attitudes or enduring feelings.

Thus an essential question in distinguishing between honesty and truth is whether the feeling of the moment recurs and persists. Are my feelings of the moment durable? Or are they simply consequences of temporary threat, whether imagined or real? Are they based on what is actually happening here and now? Or are these feelings continuations and projections of what occurred several minutes ago, perhaps in another situation or with another person? Have I simply projected and transferred feelings from another time and place? One way of knowing the truth is to wait. Do the feelings remain? Are they continuous? When I tested these questions, I found that in most instances my anger dissipated when I waited. The moment was not potent enough, not sufficiently evocative, to continue to push within for expression. Or, the old feeling carried forward disappeared, and I could then experience my real self in the present moment. The new awareness was simple enough: Being true to myself was more important than being honest with myself. Honesty has a here-now value, but truth represents something basic and enduring, something that brings coherence and unity to past, present, and future. Honesty of the moment has a significance in its own right; but an honesty which also endures and connects with the integral in me, rather than the peripheral, is much more satisfying and growth-evoking, and thus represents a true value for me. I choose truth, not honesty, when I am being most fully myself.

The following distinctions have now come to be important in my awareness of the issues behind honesty vs. truth:

Truth and honesty are related but basically different phenomena and values. Honesty is true if it is authentic to the moment and consistent with the basic self of the person. Honesty is essentially a lie when it is momentary and inconsistent with the self of the person. If I am honest when I am not myself and being myself is the truth, then I am lying when I am being honest. The mask I am wearing is an honest mask when I reveal it, but it is still a mask. The true me is beneath the mask and has continuity, substance, and endurance.

Honesty is a relative value. Truth is an enduring value. Romantic love is honest but it is not true. Love that undergoes the tests of time, crisis, and change and continues to exist is true love. A temporary, honest relationship has value, but the relationship that deepens into friendship and becomes a true meeting of persons is of incomparable, lasting value. Honesty refers only to myself; it is my feeling, in this moment, with this person. Thus it is a self-centered concern. Truth takes into account the total situation. Truth includes the other—his feeling, his state of being. The choice I make in honesty is a response to my own momentary feeling, but the choice I make in truth considers the other person's life and his readiness to receive my communication. Anger that is honest may become compassion if I am concerned with the other, if I am seeking a level of truth that will satisfy the requirement of the total situation. Whether or not I express a feeling of the moment, when truth is at stake, I take into account the implications and consequences of my communication in the lives of the persons involved. If the "honest" expression does not enable the persons and the relationship to move forward, does not facilitate real dialogue, it can lead to repetitive battles and frozen attitudes.

I am honest if I say I do not want to do something but am willing to try it out. In the doing, if I discover that it has

meaning and value, that it fits the person I am, that it brings
a quality of life and spirit, then I connect with it and it becomes a true part of me. For me the deliberate and inten-
tional expression of anger in the moment is honest but not
necessarily true. I prefer not to devote my life with others to
painful encounters centering around anger that has but momentary value. I prefer not to make a production out of minor
annoyances. I do not want to run away from a true conflict,
but I prefer to ignore, bypass, or transcend minor issues. In
my observations I have seen honesty made a rule of expression without any regard for the spirit of life among people,
without any consideration of what people value, seek, and
experience in relating and growing with one another.

When I confront another person I must be aware both of
my honest responses to the moment and of the long-range
truth. These values may be in conflict. If they are, I always
have a choice. If I am seeking the deepest level of communication and the highest level of health, then I choose the
enduring not the momentary. Sometimes anger will take me
there, if rooted in something deep and real; but more often
by waiting, by letting the moment reach a fullness, by focus-
ing on more vital concerns and feelings within, the anger is
bypassed because it is not the significant or chosen feeling; it
is transcended for a more vital channel of communication and
relationship. If an honest feeling or response is also true, it
will recur; it will be reinforced. When it represents something
basic and solid, not tangential and fleeting, then it is worth
pursuing. In seeking the truth with reference to one's self,
there are many alternative forms of expression. If the choice
I make creates disturbance in me and in the lives of others,
then I have other possibilities, other alternatives. Each is
equally honest. To continue to use the same pattern of com-

munication because it is honest fails to recognize the equal honesty of other forms of expression. A communication that repeatedly fails to work cannot be justified on the basis of honesty. The true path enables me to continue to be who I am and at the same time facilitates the other person in being himself. Each communication I make has vitalizing potential for me and for my relations, but the true way should lead to a sense of fulfillment, to actualizing myself, and in so doing make it possible for others to actualize themselves.

8 | *to struggle*
between honesty
and compassion

In this chapter, I shall discuss the struggle that occurs when two values of equal importance—honesty and compassion—are in conflict, the struggle that takes place within me, in silence and in dialogue, in becoming more fully aware of the meaning of the moment, in making a choice, and in putting my decision into action. When I use "honesty" in this chapter, it is not the fleeting or distorted honesty discussed in the previous chapter but rather honesty consistent with the real me, which is based on what is actual and what continues to be relevant in my experience.

When I consider the problems I have faced during the past year, none has more fully engrossed me than the choice between honesty and compassion when each is alive in me, and yet at odds. The choice is simple when there is no conflict or when a conflict exists but the other person is not suffering. But when the person is in pain and I am experiencing both compassion and feelings that would confront and challenge the other person, then I face a complicated inner struggle. Sometimes I express these opposing feelings and they shake and disturb the other person. Sometimes by staying fully with myself and entering into dialogue, the confrontation deepens the relationship and moves it toward a more complete life.

Even in the presence of the anxiety, pain, and suffering of other persons, I value the honesty which is an expression of one's real self; without it reality may be distorted and growth deterred. Honesty characterizes the person and enables him to create an identity, to communicate a real presence, and to establish authentic bonds with others. The individual increasingly comes to know who he is through the stand he takes when he expresses his ideas, values, beliefs, and convictions, and through the declaration and ownership of his feelings. Being honest is a direct way of introducing one's self. The net effect of continuous, real honesty is the awareness and recognition of one's particularity and individuality. As a result, new potentials are opened and awakened; the person is alive and his presence is felt—whether that aliveness takes the form of outward assertiveness or inner serenity. Thus, to be honest is simply to be. Without honesty there is no actual being present; there is no flow of life and no possibility for new life. In its most basic form, honesty has to do with one's own self, one's own feelings, perceptions, moment-to-moment experiencing. It is the direct communication of the actuality of one's being. In honesty, one does not explain or interpret the feelings of others but refers solely to one's own experiencing.

Buber's position on honesty is illuminating: "Whatever the meaning of the word 'truth' may be in other realms, in the interhuman realm it means that men communicate themselves to one another as what they are. It does not depend on one saying to the other everything that occurs to him, but only on his letting no seeming creep in between himself and the other. It does not depend on one letting himself go before another, but on granting to the man to whom he communicates himself a share in his being. This is a question of the authenticity of the interhuman, and where this is not to be found, neither is the human element itself authentic." [1]

In contrast, compassion is more fully connected to the other person's self. And though self and other may merge in a situation of severe pain and suffering, nevertheless the center of the experience is sustained and determined by the other person's crisis. To feel compassion is to be within the other person's world and experience his pain and despair. In its positive form compassion involves a presence and an affirmation, an expression of deep sympathy and regard. In its negative form compassion can become condescension, a kind of pity for one less favored, for one who lives an inferior life. There is a right way to express and experience compassion so that the other person is not reduced in any way, but rather maintains a feeling of equality and is thereby helped to bear his suffering, to live with it and grow from it. The compassionate person helps the other realize (not in words but in the actuality of his presence) that suffering is not reduced by refusing to face it or by wallowing in it but only by accepting it, surrendering to it, and letting the natural healing processes take root and unfold. When this happens, the other person may become more sensitive, aware, and deepened in his perceptions and feelings. In *The Method of Zen*, Herrigel touches the essence of what I am attempting to communicate,

> The real meaning of suffering discloses itself only to him who has learned the art of compassion. . . . Gradually he

1. Martin Buber, *Between Man and Man*, trans. Ronald Gregor Smith (Boston: Beacon Press, 1955), p. 77.

will fall silent, and in the end will sit there wordless, for a long time sunk deep in himself. And the strange thing is that this silence is not felt by the other person as indifference, as a desolate emptiness which disturbs rather than calms. It is as if this silence had more meaning than countless words could ever have. It is as if he were being drawn into a field of force from which fresh strength flows into him. He feels suffused with a strange confidence. . . . And it may be that in these hours, the resolve will be born to set out on the path that turns a wretched existence into a life of happiness.[2]

Like honesty, compassion may be expressed through verbal means but its basic form of communication is silence.

I know from my own experience that in a crisis with family, friends, or colleagues, it is possible to feel compassionately present and at the same time to be honestly in conflict with the other person. Sometimes, the issue is barely perceptible yet the struggle and the battle to remain true to my total self are enormously real.

Just now in concentrating on this conflict, I am reminded of an encounter with Bob. Again and again he experienced betrayal and perfidy in his relationships. Often as he sat with me he related his feelings of loneliness and isolation, the defeat and failure of his every effort to experience success in love relationships, his disillusionment with every potential friendship. He felt his life to be ebbing away, felt himself growing older and more desperate. I can envision him turning to me, appealing, sometimes demanding to be rescued from his lonely prison. I reach out to him, feeling the agony of his struggle. For a moment we touch but soon he lashes

2. Eugen Herrigel, *The Method of Zen*, ed. by Hermann Tausend, trans. by R. F. C. Hull (New York: Pantheon Books, Inc., 1960), pp. 124–25.

out at me, fighting against his own tender feelings with a frozen smile and a barrage of sarcasm. He signals with his body: he pushes me away and yet expresses a faint lingering hope that I will stay with him no matter what he says or does. I find it difficult to become the object of his sneering smile and his cold violent words that are used to batter and torture. At the same time, I sense the soft, fragile, human quality but it is so deeply buried that I must strain to feel it. From what he has shared, I recognize the familiar pattern: the hungering for affirmation and, at the same time, the desire to crush and destroy whatever touches him. The tenderness is the most suspect; the firm, hard, cold, bargaining compromise can be trusted. At first the lashing is a shock but I am learning to live with it, silently, knowing that this is his journey, that whatever else may happen between us, for awhile I must follow him on his own path. I feel deep compassion for his lonely presence and for his suffering. I am, for the most part, responding with sympathy but occasionally another feeling emerges in me. After numerous assaults, something pulls inside me and demands that I encounter him. For an instant I struggle with the choice: To continue to express the compassion I feel for his pain, or to communicate my feeling that he is making his own prison and condemning me for not rescuing him from it. Which path should I take: Should I share with him my own hurt in being unjustly criticized? Should I sympathize with his anger when he has endured one more rejection or express my own feelings of rejection when he castigates me and belittles my efforts to help him?

Sometimes, in the whole of my being, I am unconditionally with him in his suffering; but at other times while still feeling the emptiness of his life I also sense the poverty of our relationship. Which means more to Bob, my compassionate pres-

ence or my protests against his self-centered pronouncements? Which do I believe in more—the supportive and
affirming dimension of me or the actively confronting? Both
are true aspects of my being; both are honest. Each has its
place in my relationship with Bob but it is sometimes a struggle to know which will facilitate and which will interfere.

There are times in my relations with others when I feel
squelched, denied, unrecognized—regarded primarily as a
helper who is sympathetic and affirming. Another side breaks
out into the open, and I express a component of me that has
been dormant; a dimension of my own being is thrust forward
in conflict with the other person. Almost inevitably, the pain
I create is intense and my honesty turns into another kind of
compassion. I am deeply sympathizing with the person I
have just hurt. But the point has been made; a new aspect of
me has registered strongly in the other person. The message
comes through and a change begins to take place. Without
in any way becoming the focus or center of the relationship,
all ensuing communications are affected by that change.
When honesty of this kind serves both persons, awarenesses
and understandings are being created. The conflict has under-
gone a test of love and the persons perceive one another in a
new way. Even their glances contain a unique light that
comes from having weathered a threatening, potentially fatal
form of interpersonal communication. But when it does not
work in a positive way, full, honest expression at a time when
a person is suffering adds to the pain, threatens him, and may
seriously jeopardize a return to a full life and an openness to
new experience. Having sunk deeply into despair and having
shared it with another person, the challenge of an honest
encounter may come as a sudden blow. The flow of feeling
is stopped; the person closes up and regrets having revealed

the depth of his anguish. He now begins to check his feelings, control them, guardedly select what he can safely communicate.

The compassionate approach does not use honesty as a weapon but as an attitude or perspective that recognizes the importance of responding uniquely to the compelling nature of each situation. The problem becomes one of discovering the healthy path to take, the human way to enhance the lives of the persons involved. Being compassionate and not confronting when another dimension of one's being is at odds with the person may not be fully honest but still consistent with a higher value, consistent with a truth that enables the persons involved to maintain their integrity and to continue on a workable path together. The confrontation may actually best serve the persons and the relationship; it may be the catalyst to new awareness and growth. Neither honesty nor compassion can be chosen automatically; ultimately the choice must be authentic and valued in terms of the immediate situation and in terms of becoming life.

Another factor in the struggle between compassion and honesty has to do with the significance of the issue. In many instances the contradictory feelings may not be strong enough or important enough to override compassion. Then, I can let the thought or feeling stand while still remaining sensitive and responsive to the other person. As the meeting with the other person unfolds, the feeling may dissipate completely; the issue is naturally settled. To make minor contradictions central means engaging in irrelevancies that interfere with the growth potential of the persons and the relationship.

When the vital issues are met and struggled with, when they lead to real connections between persons, minor aggravations no longer matter. The tone of a voice that once irritated me no longer stands out, or if it does it may even be valued. When compassionate responses to central matters do not eliminate the conflicting feelings, they can be faced through encounter; but the challenge should occur in a human context, in a relationship where the battle is waged with commitment and concern.

Ultimately truth must come from one's own self however compelling the "honesty" of the other person or the group. Honest, sensitive feedback at appropriate moments may facilitate this process—especially if it serves to bring the person back to his own senses, to his own self. Otherwise, there is a danger that the individual will lose his own direction and cease to be able to guide his own fate and destiny. Buber expresses a similar concern in the following passage:

> To-day host upon host of men have everywhere sunk into the slavery of collectives, and each collective is the supreme authority for its own slaves; there is no longer, superior to the collectives, any universal sovereignty in idea, faith, or spirit. Against the values, decrees and decisions of the collective no appeal is possible. This is true, not only for the totalitarian countries, but also for the parties and party-like groups in the so-called democracies. Men who have so lost themselves to the collective Moloch cannot be rescued from it by any reference, however eloquent, to the absolute whose kingdom the Moloch has usurped. One has to begin by pointing to that sphere where man himself, in the hours of utter solitude, occasionally becomes aware of the disease through sudden pain; by pointing to the relation of the individual to his own self. In order to enter into a personal relation with the absolute, it is first necessary to be a person again, to rescue one's real personal self from the fiery jaws of collectivism which devours all self-hood. The desire to do

this is latent in the pain the individual suffers through his distorted relation to his own self.[3]

The importance of honesty and compassion was revealed to me recently in my experience with Mike with whom I spent three hours following a brief encounter group experience. He had been bitingly attacked by college classmates who told him they were being honest with him for the first time. As Mike related the experience, he said "they" had condemned his sense of humor; they regarded it as phony, inappropriate, and a cover-up for feelings of inferiority and self-doubt. What "they" did not realize was that Mike regarded his ability to see humor in almost every situation as his only asset, his only feature that could interest and attract others. He felt that his humor gave him uniqueness and character and provided an opening to others. In my three-hour session with him he cried continually, in agony, repeatedly screaming "Oh why did I ever come here. They all think I'm so superficial. There's nothing to me. Nothing! They all know it now. I don't know what to do with myself. I don't know what I am anymore. I can never face them again." I listened as he spoke of his family, the alienation at home, and how his humor had saved him many times from psychic death. Without it he did not know who he could become. After considerable painful searching and self-condemnation, he suddenly grew quiet. I felt the crisis of total breakdown had passed. We sat silently for quite a while; then he suggested we take a walk. It was a beautiful fall day and something in the wind, in the changing colors of the trees and in the blowing leaves, as well as in the feeling of intimacy between us, changed Mike's mood. The anxiety attack diminished and he began to

3. Buber, *Between Man and Man*, pp. 110–111.

speak calmly. The experience with nature had been more
restorative, more self-awakening than the group confrontation. He decided to return to his group and asked that I join
him for a while. Within minutes he fell asleep and slept
peacefully the rest of the afternoon. I think each person in
his group had learned that there are times when honesty
should be tempered with compassion.

A quotation from James Baldwin captures the spirit of my
message:

> The moment we cease to hold each other,
> the moment we break faith with one another
> the sea engulfs us and the light goes out.

9 | *loneliness and love*

Almost ten years ago I published a book, part of which focused on the loneliness of hospitalized children, on their initial fear of abandonment and fear of the unknown. I saw children who were imprisoned and confined protest and rebel. Their vigorous expressions soon changed to despair and apathy as the doctors, nurses, and aides went to work on them. What shocked me then and still shocks me is that competent, well-trained professional people can unwittingly kill the sources of life, stifle genuine human expression, and crush the human spirit. I saw people manipulate healthy protest into "acceptable" behavior. The official spokesmen of our society still delude themselves into believing that people have made a good adjustment when they become docile, "cooperative," and submissive to rules and regulations contrary to healthy human life. Rebellion against dehumanizing people and experiences, against authoritarian devices and pressures, is a positive sign that a particular human being is alive. When protests against violence and alienation are blocked, when resources for self-expression are eliminated, when opportunities for real encounters are denied, loneliness is a natural human response. It is a force within, a struggle to maintain one's integrity and wholeness in the face of indifference, unresponsiveness, manipulation, and meaningless communication.

Increasingly, I have become painfully aware of the terribleness of most communication: of people talking but not saying what they mean; of the contradiction between the outward words and expressions and the inner meanings and messages; of people looking as if they were listening without any real connection or contact with one another. When I am with such persons I experience deep feelings of loneliness, and I want to break through the empty words and come into touch with the feelings; I want to go beyond the icebergs on top, and into what is actually happening deep down. I have become keenly aware that individuals rarely express what really matters: the tender, shy, reluctant feelings, the sensitive, fragile, intense feelings. Too often we receive the words but not the concrete, actual messages and meanings. What has happened to us as human beings that we can be so near and yet so far, that we can be so distant from each other and not even know? Where are we anyway in those hours when the human spirit cries out in despair, when the hunger for sharing and for loving comes through in disguised and devious forms? What has happened when we have become so radically cut off from our own humanity that we kill the human need for compassion and understanding, when the longing for response is not even recognized or noticed?

Somehow I wish that in first meetings people would communicate only in gestures and in other nonverbal ways. If we would just stop in the midst of our verbal exchanges; if by some force we were required to remain silent, then perhaps we would find our way back to real persons, to actual, concrete experiences, to direct communication, to the deep regions of the self. To know the potential of human compassion and love and to see the fragmentary communications between man and man—that for me is utterly lonely. If we could all just stop and really listen to one another, really hear—not what's on the surface but in the depth of being.

I do not mean that I am finished with this challenge. I am constantly struggling—especially in the loneliness of love, where I am often astray, lost, missing the potential depth of a relaitonship. Suddenly it hits me and I am aware of just missing the person, almost coming into touch; but like a shadow or filter, in the instant of recognition something happens, something evades and comes between. Is it pride, habit, ego, self-esteem? This is how I felt when suddenly I became aware that Mary and I had drifted apart and I had not even noticed—not even noticed the difference—because the daily words we exchanged were the same. Everything looked normal but all of a sudden I realized that I was missing her—yes, I was seeing her every day and missing her. I was not experiencing the new person growing up, the new world unfolding in her, her sudden discovery of all kinds of feelings and thoughts, the soaring moments and the dark and depressing colors and tones. I had been listening, listening to every word she spoke but I hadn't heard the becoming child growing into youth; I hadn't recognized the significance of changes in her perceptions of people, school, family, and society. Most significantly, I hadn't recognized the changes within her: all the critical dimensions of her world. She just couldn't put all of this into words. But one day it became so unbearable—her loneliness, her inability to share her feeling that I had pulled away from her; one day it just came in a torrent of feeling and we talked and talked and a great burden came between us which new words could not resolve. The love that was in our hearts was stuck deep down. She couldn't explain anymore, she couldn't talk anymore; but somehow, somehow, suddenly from my utterly dense state, at the very bottom of my own loneliness, in this love, I heard —I really heard her disillusionment, her disenchantment, and her loss of innocence. I realized then that words could not settle anything but only silence, touch, and the depth of feeling between us.

By some miracle, my sense of responsibility as a person of authority melted away and all that mattered was Mary's unique existence and the importance, the necessity, of my knowing her in this new existence. In that instant I stopped hanging onto my old image and I began to know Mary. Among other things, this entailed listening, hearing, and— gradually, slowly—learning to appreciate some of the centers of her world that had become so alien to me. I know now that the relationship itself is more spontaneous, stronger, and that the crisis and the suffering have helped create new bonds between us. What was essential is beautifully expressed in Raymond Baughan's poem:

> What is required of us in our time
> is that we go down
> into uncertainty
> where what is new is old as every morning,
> and what is well known is not known as well.
>
> That we go down
> into the most human
> where living men have vanished
> and the music of their meaning
> has been trapped and sealed.

What is asked of us in our time
is that we break open
our blocked caves
and find each other.

Nothing less will heal the anguished spirit,
nor release the heart to act in love.[1]

Love involves the willingness to face the inevitable pain and doubt, the inevitable misunderstanding and dark moments. Other feelings arise—doubt, despair, disillusionment—from the rhythms of living and dying; people come into one another's lives for brief periods and go their separate ways. Each year I am separated from people I have met and come to love. Especially painful are the relations with students with whom I have struggled to create a meaningful life. Just as we begin to live in a full way, we have to depart and face the challenge of beginning again with other people, in other places and times.

I experienced a particularly painful separation recently. As I walked down the hall, I suddenly remembered footsteps from my past—quick, joyful footsteps—and I saw, really saw, faces of many persons I had come to know. Sometimes as we passed, we touched, if only for a brief moment; that touch contained a warm glow of greeting and affirmation and the recognition of being alive and caring, of sharing something vital in each other's lives. Sometimes only our eyes met but in our glances was something strong, direct, unwaivering. We felt with our eyes; our hearts soared; we *knew* and that knowing carried a special message that brightened the day. Communication, both silent and in dialogue, although brief, was

1. Raymond John Baughan, *The Sound of Silence* (Boston: Dept. of Publications UUA, 1965), p. 7.

complete. In these encounters were tingling sensations of excitement and warmth, and the simple joy of meeting someone
real. Whatever the mood of the moment—happiness, frivol-
ity, sorrow—we met in honest ways; we became increasingly
free with one another to speak or to remain silent, to touch or
to pass by quietly. We let the temper of our hearts speak
openly and rejoiced in human fellowship.

Where are those sounds and movements of love and life
now? The halls are deadly silent. Faces no longer appear. An
important pattern of living has ended. It is difficult to
breathe. I am separated; I am alone. I can feel the loneliness
of a living, breathing world that I helped to create and became totally involved in, that no longer exists. Somehow I
must let go of that world in which I was once firmly rooted.
But how? To be alive, to be human, to create life, to com-
mune with others, to know the depth of dialogue—and then
suddenly to face only the dark, cold, quiet emptiness of floors
and walls and ceilings.

I rush out into the wind where I can breathe again, where
there is earth and sky and space. I search for my place among
the trees; I find a steady, quiet, continuing presence where I
can reach out for shade or warmth, and reach in for the
strength to create new dreams. For a short while in the sun I
feel this new world coming. I know it is there but the intense
feelings of loneliness return and I hurry away.

From past experience I know that a new world is coming,
a world in which I can laugh and love freely; but at the moment, it is only a remote and fleeting awareness that does not
stop the lonely feelings. I knew then in the midst of the joy
of creating a rich life with others that one day it would end,
that I would experience feelings of isolation and loss. Yet
each day came and went and I lived in it as if it would last

forever. If I had not let these persons fully enter my life, I would not know these desolate feelings. But I always make this choice. For me there is no other way to live, so I stay with the lonely feelings and wonder how many more new worlds are in me to create.

Out of the dying, a new life is born, following each good-bye, a real hello. This poem of Baughan's says it well:

> Some worlds end—
> the little one
> you lived in as a child,
> the crazy one
> men make of self and pain,
> the one that is your breath.
>
> The years turn under;
> tides and seasons run;
> but sunlight's here,
> the smell of sea,
> and hope in human hearts.[2]

A whole new world opened for me when I discovered that sometimes the only way to meet a person is in his lonely depths. This is my dream now: to find the person underneath the mask, to reach for this unique potential, and to develop feelings of human compassion. I am thinking here of the loneliness of pain and anguish in associating with people who are playing roles; of the loneliness of human interaction in which the possibilities for intimacy, communion, and love are dormant and unrealized; of lives filled with too many words, pictures, social scenes, and sounds. I am thinking of people who know the peacefulness and beauty of lonely solitude, of the

2. Ibid., p. 14.

rising and setting sun, of the stars, of the trees and flowers
that grow strikingly in their own way, or the suffering that
comes into all relationships.

> "Let me tell you something very important. . . ." says
> Monsignor Meredith in *The Devil's Advocate*. "It is no new
> thing to be lonely. It comes to all of us sooner or later.
> Friends die, families die. Lovers and husbands, too. We get
> old, we get sick. And the last and greatest loneliness is
> death, which I am facing now. There are no pills to cure
> that. No formulas to charm it away. It's a condition of men
> that we can't escape. If we try to retreat from it, we end
> in a darker hell. . . . But if we face it, if we remember that
> there are a million others like us, if we try to reach out to
> comfort them and not ourselves, we find in the end that we
> are lonely no longer. We are in a new family, the family of
> man. . . ." [3]

I want to feel with you into the nature of loneliness, especially the loneliness of interpersonal relations: the loneliness
of listening to a person and not hearing what he says; of being
with a person who speaks words automatically and mechani-
cally while actually referring to beautiful or devastating experiences; of being with people who neither listen nor hear,
or who listen but do not actually hear; of being with people
who have significant stories to relate but who chatter on, saying the appropriate things in the appropriate ways. I want
somehow to say what it feels like to be with a person and not
really know the person—not really be aware of the actual
human presence of one self to another self—as expressed in
this letter-poem from David Gilbert of Michigan State Uni-
versity:

3. Morris L. West, *The Devil's Advocate* (New York: Dell Publishing
Co., Inc., 1959), pp. 334–35.

And were you cold
The night I sat beside you and did not take your hand
And did a coldness touch you longlow and sink to where
    you swallowed so I could not tell if a kiss burned deep
      the down dear
And was that a prayer that did not reach your lips as I bent
    to take my things from you.
Our eyes
    meeting above
      the pale white coffee cups
And what was the look you didn't turn round to give me
As I left
    and walked off to—
      for all you knew—
        another girl
And amid all the people
Did you feel half as lonely as I
    who
Wishing to feel and wanting to
    want to stay
      stayed until my hypocrisy rose, choking
And I went out to that cold night
    where nothing was there to feel
except a sometime imagined coldness
Which was not as cold or comfortless
    as my damned numbered soul.

And this from Karen Underwood, a high school senior:

The one I love has eyes that I long to make a part of my own
But when I try to look into them . . . I cannot
For there is no depth.
Only a mirror that reflects the image of my own love:
I reach out for him . . . and I am not rejected,
But merely mimicked.

He is not unkind to me.
But in his eyes I see no love . . . only obligation;
And when upon seeing this, tears creep forth,
There is no understanding . . . only question.

His lips smile and he speaks kind words of condolence.
I listen to his voice.
And I am almost persuaded to believe his words
But only his eyes tell the truth.
And I must listen.

And the loneliness created by parents who do not know,
who do not understand, the nature of love:

The time when I felt lonely was when mother had a talk
with dad. My mother talked about my pet turtle, Carl. They
wanted me to let him and his friends go. About a week after
that my dad took me out to a lake and I had my turtles with
me. I let the turtles go, and all the turles went but Carl. He
followed me along the shore. Then we walked up toward
the car; Carl followed us—then my dad threw him in the
lake. Ever since I've been feeling as if the world was leaving me.

And this yearning, hungry search of Margarethe Wiest:

I
am a
conformist, they say.
I love what they think
I should.
I am doing just what is
expected.
O God! Let them notice me.

> Draw upon me fully
> I do so want to
> rise.

Or this painful cry of Peter DeVries as he stands at the hospital bedside of his daughter and cannot reach her in the agonizing breathing of her final moments:

> Then I touched the stigmata one by one: the prints of the needles, the wound in the breast that had for so many months now scarcely ever closed. I caressed the perfectly shaped head. I bent to kiss the cheeks, the breast that would now never be fulfilled, that no youth would ever touch. "Oh, my lamb."
> The lips curled in another smile, one whose secret I thought I knew. I recognized it without the aid of the gaze, now sealed forever from mine, with which it had come to me so often throughout her childhood. It was the expression on her face when her homework was going well, the shine of pride at a column of figures mastered or a poem . . . successfully forged. It was the smile of satisfaction worn at the piano when a new composition had been memorized, on her bicycle when, gripping its vanquished horns, she had ridden past me on her first successful solo around the yard. . . .
> But this time the experience was not to be shared. She was going alone. Even without the eyes to help communicate it, there was a glow of the most intense concentration on her face, with that wariness of error or shortcoming that had always made it so complete and so characteristic. She had never seemed more alive than now, when she was gathering all the life within her for the proper discharge of whatever this last assignment might have been. . . . I bent again to whisper a question in her ear, but there was no

> answer—only the most remote sense of flight upon the face.
> It shone like a star about to burst and, in bursting, yield me
> all its light at once—could I but bear the gift.[4]

Sometimes it is necessary to transcend the words, to go
beyond them, to hear underneath and find the great euphoric
moments, the joy, the glory, the anguish, and the suffering—
yes, and to hear also the cruelty, the anger, the rejection, and
the betrayal of man. And, having heard, it is necessary at
times to reach beyond these feelings, to sense the real meanings, and to follow one's intuitions beyond the immediate.
Essential, formative, fundamental experiences leave indelible
traces within us—feelings that are carried forth as powerful
reminders of human viciousness, deceit, and hypocrisy, as
well as reminders of human courage, love, beauty, and tenderness. To meet the real person, it is essential that we know
what exists in the person—what he is living and experiencing
with other human beings, what he is actually feeling—but it
is also essential to move beyond into the unknown, to transcend the past and discover new meaning in the present and
in the future.

At another time and in another place, my words came back
to me in a letter from Howard, who—after years of fighting
against his loneliness and denying it as a sick component of
himself—discovered that his suffering had a meaning and
that he could live with it because it was a part of his own self.
He had known loneliness all his life: rejected by his family,
denied his own unique heritage, forced into interests and
goals that were alienating, he struggled at last through loneliness to his own identity. And though this meant pain and
anguish at times, it also meant that his life now had meaning,

4. Peter DeVries, *The Blood of the Lamb* (Boston: Little, Brown and
Company, 1961), pp. 234–35.

that his own self was his contribution to life, that his presence in the world was all he could offer but that this was enough, that this was everything—unique, intense, incomparable, never before or never again to be. It was just this meaning which changed the entire world in which he lived.

To be known in this way was what I had awakened to: to perceive the world from vast, expansive inner openings and new pathways; to see light where there had been darkness; to find beauty in broken bits of stone; to see color where all had been dingy and gray; to hear a human voice and absorb a smile; to recognize the brevity of life and the necessity of making each moment count; to realize the ecstasy of human companionship. When someone cares enough to see into the deepest roots of one's nature, though it is heart-rending to be known in this naked sense, it brings the deepest measure of unique and thrilling sensations.

The absolute meanings of human companionship and of the loneliness of relationship are often missed. In a recent seminar, Roberta especially haunted me. In words, she related how she had been uprooted in two wars in Germany, seen her home destroyed twice, barely escaping herself, carrying within her memories of time once shared, of happy moments once known. How could she ever really laugh again or weep again or let herself feel deeply any real feelings, for there underneath any experience was man's degradation, the danger of annihilation, and the horror and pain of having thirty members of her family cruelly destroyed. Curtis followed these statements with some of his own. And it was as if Roberta had not spoken at all. Curtis' response was that he too had been through two wars; his father and brother had been killed and other members of his family permanently maimed and diminished. While they were evening the score, I became sick inside, sick in thought and feeling for these two people who had once been alive and who had been cruelly numbed by their experiences. Now as they spoke to each other they were more dead than alive.

In *Miracles*, Lynette Joass, a twelve-year-old girl from New Zealand, expresses the same concern:

> Dark, dark night.
> The trees. The river.
> One more day;
> For so slow goes the day.
> Before the end
>   the world goes round
>   once more.
> The world begins the day.
> The night has gone.
> The day for the end of the world
>   once more begins.
> Once more begins the sun
> Slow, so slow.
> Go on, world, live.
> Begin, sweet sun.
> Begin, sweet world.
>   The people live and die.
>   people die alive
>   alive
>   alive.[5]

Roberta and Curtis had spoken in dead moments; they exchanged only words—of atrocity, of death, of destruction. What actually passed between them? How it hurt to sense the depth of suffering, to want to bridge the distance between

5. Richard Lewis, ed., *Miracles* (New York: Simon & Schuster, Inc., 1966), p. 182.

them but to see no way until sometime later when love itself broke through the long sleepless nights and the visions and terrors of the past, when love transcended the barriers that existed between them and enabled them to meet person-to-person.

That night, I realized so clearly how some of my most lonely experiences were connected with love: from the first shocking discovery of myself as an essentially lonely person to my awareness of my love for Mary and the inability to break the barriers to communication and to find her in that pain and anguish and horror in which she lived for awhile. Yes, and nearly all the other love relationships—the separations, the misunderstandings, the quarrels, and even the joy and the beauty and the happiness of love. There are times when that very love for a person makes it difficult to be on good terms with loneliness.

Among those lonely experiences is the feeling of being pulled in opposite directions by forces of love, like the child who is caught in the battles and conflicts of his parents, each of whom is pulling him. He loves, he really loves, both persons but he feels helpless to express this love and to reach his parents, without denying one or the other. A similar feeling of loneliness is experienced by the person who is caught between two friends who are attacking one another with words, hurting one another with deliberate phrasings, picking, needling, pushing.

To be aware of love, in its real sense, is loneliness: the hopes, the joys, the ecstasy, all the tensions of loss and fulfillment, of dreams and despair; this awareness that love is now and yet passing, that one reaches out to hold the moment and suddenly it is gone, suddenly it is sealed in the past, in memories, to be recaptured in reminiscence—the knowledge that this love can never exist again. It is the loneliness of returning to the town in which one lived as a child and feeling only the thin ghosts of that existence and not the substance; the loneliness of wanting longingly, fervently to recapture the feelings or just to feel but not to be able to feel and to know only distance and detachment. This feeling is beautifully expressed in Donna Turley's book *Mosaic of My Self:*

> The loss, the missing, the emptiness . . . it is all inevitable to one who lives and gives. The longing for all those I love, the half-dying for want of that old touch or glance . . . that same familiar knowingness and those hands and eyes . . . which so many past times saw and felt and knew me. Those brows once so often knitted with my pain and sorrow and those worn hands which once held so much that was dear to me . . . which once were within my own reach . . . and I could take them and hold them as tightly and as long as I wished . . . now where are they? Where could I go to gather together all my loves and all my caring ones and all the pieces of my gifts, and all my sources of strength? [6]

It is a continual challenge to come to terms with these feelings of despair, somehow to express something of this almost overwhelming agony. The words that immediately come to me are "a deadness of spirit," a kind of inner dying and the pain of seeing ongoing life, being in touch with it, sensitive and caring, yet deep down a decaying spirit, growing out of the feeling of being fragmented and torn by the impossibility of continually maintaining one's own individuality, by the impossibility of living in different worlds at the same time and fervently wanting to be in touch with everyone—yes, to be,

6. Donna Turley, *Mosaic of My Self* (Cambridge: Howard A. Doyle Publishing Company, 1968), p. 8.

to see, to feel, to love everyone. It is the impossibility of being with the one and with the other, without somehow losing one's self; of being pulled and divided by loyalties, split by forces outside, yet somehow transcending the divisiveness, staying with one's self and remaining true to one's own being.

Suffering and anguish, while being lived, can be almost unbearable; but, in time, through a mysterious process of awareness and transcendence, the hurt moves forward into the bliss of liberation and into a new zest for living. Then there is a passionate claim to human existence that brings with it a feeling of relationship. The self that does not reach out to encounter and include others is, indeed, still mourning, still split and suffering. To come back to the human community, one must know the agony of broken communications, of unanswered doubts and questions; one must know the clear visions of loneliness and solitude and the joy of being born again. One must also know the depths of loving unconditionally and of being unconditionally loved, of forming new bonds with others that cancel out pettiness, misunderstanding, meanness, and incomprehension: one must know the feeling of genuine communication and unity.

These realizations come, not by forceful actions against others, but by a retreat within, through the engagement with oneself in which the intensity and depth of feelings are experienced. Realization comes through a process of meditation and open inquiry in which a new path opens whereby the individual can return to life with others. From the lonely struggle the person experiences a new determination, a resolve to confront life actively with the full presence of the self. Loneliness is an inevitable outcome of real love, but it is also a process through which new love becomes possible. Love which is genuine is its own thing. It is unique, incomparable, true only as itself. And because real love is unique, it is inescapably lonely. In the alive person, the rhythms of loneliness and love deepen and enrich human existence. The lonely experience gives a person back to himself, affirms his identity, and enables him to take steps toward new life. The experience of love is the spark and energy of excitement and joy; it is what makes friendship a lifetime value and what makes activity purposeful. A balance is essential. Exaggeration of either loneliness or love leads to self-denial and despair. Love has no meaning without loneliness; loneliness becomes real only as a response to love.

references

BAUGHAN, RAYMOND JOHN. *The Sound of Silence*. Boston: Department of Publications, Unitarian Universalist Assn., 1965.

DEVRIES, PETER. *The Blood of the Lamb*. Boston: Little, Brown and Company, 1961.

LEWIS, RICHARD, ed. *Miracles*. New York: Simon & Schuster, Inc., 1966.

MALCOLM X. *Autobiography*. New York: Grove Press, Inc., 1965.

MOUSTAKAS, CLARK. *Individuality and Encounter*. Cambridge, Mass.: Howard Doyle Publishing Co., 1968.

TURLEY, DONNA LEE. *Mosaic of My Self*. Cambridge, Mass.: Howard Doyle Publishing Co., 1968.

WEST, MORRIS L. *The Devil's Advocate*. New York: William Morrow & Co., Inc., 1959.